BANJO CAMP!

LEARNING, PICKING & JAMMING

with BLUEGRASS and OLD-TIME GREATS

Zhenya Gene Senyak

LARK BOOKS

A Division of Sterling Publishing Co., Inc.

New York / London

SENIOR EDITOR
Deborah Morgenthal

ART DIRECTOR
Thom Gaines

ILLUSTRATORS
Dana Irwin
Jason Krekel
Zhenya Gene Senyak

COVER DESIGNER
4 Eyes Design

Library of Congress Cataloging-in-Publication Data

Senyak, Zhenya Gene.
  Banjo camp! : learning, picking & jamming with bluegrass & old-time greats / Zhenya Gene Senyak. -- 1st ed.
      p. cm.
  Includes index.
  ISBN 978-1-60059-282-9 (pb with cd : alk. paper)
  1. Banjo--United States--History. 2. Banjoists--United States. 3. Bluegrass music--History and criticism. I. Title.
  ML1015.B3S46 2008
  787.8'816420973--dc22

                              2008019845

10 9 8 7 6 5 4 3 2 1

First Edition

Published by Lark Books, A Division of
Sterling Publishing Co., Inc.
387 Park Avenue South, New York, NY 10016

Text © 2008, Zhenya Gene Senyak
Photography © 2008, Zhenya Gene Senyak, unless otherwise specified
Illustrations © 2008, Lark Books, unless otherwise specified

Distributed in Canada by Sterling Publishing,
c/o Canadian Manda Group, 165 Dufferin Street
Toronto, Ontario, Canada M6K 3H6

Distributed in the United Kingdom by GMC Distribution Services,
Castle Place, 166 High Street, Lewes, East Sussex, England BN7 1XU

Distributed in Australia by Capricorn Link (Australia) Pty Ltd.,
P.O. Box 704, Windsor, NSW 2756 Australia

If you have questions or comments about this book, please contact:
Lark Books
67 Broadway
Asheville, NC 28801
828-253-0467

Manufactured in China

ISBN 13: 978-1-60059-282-9

For information about custom editions, special sales, premium and corporate purchases, please contact Sterling Special Sales Department at 800-805-5489 or specialsales@sterlingpub.com.

Contents

To Pete Seeger,
   for showing us the way

Author's Introduction

I didn't pick up the banjo while sitting on my grandfather's porch. I didn't have an uncle with an old country fiddle in the closet. And if not for the "Beverly Hillbillies," I wouldn't have heard bluegrass banjo until I grew up and left town.

My first banjo, a patched and cobbled-together homemade instrument, was lying on a flea-market table piled with vases, plastic flowers, and a chipped water pitcher when I discovered it just a few years ago. "You can use it as a wall decoration," the seller said.

Armed with new strings and the Pete Seeger banjo book, I learned some chords and felt an immediate affinity for this good old banjo that had, like me, seen better times and yet could still cheerfully plunk along and look forward to a promising future.

Now, banjo has become a trusted and joyful part of my everyday life. How did it happen? Along with friends, books, and teachers, a key part of my education has been banjo camp. Several, in fact. Banjo camp doesn't take the place of listening to good music and sitting down for the hard work of learning to play, but it does serve up the inspiration and exposure that make the whole process a lot easier and more natural.

And it's an idea that has caught on. Banjo camps take place all over the world, and why not? You can pretty much count on having fun while accelerating your banjo learning curve. You'll also learn to play banjo with other folks, meet other banjo players, come home with new banjo gear, cool banjo T-shirts, autographs on the head of your banjo, blisters on your fingers, and the jingle-jangle jamming sound of banjo in your ears.

Much like camp for kids, the banjo camp experience takes you out of your element. For one thing, you're carrying your banjo around a lot more than usual, and there's not much chance to check your e-mail. Once you unpack your stuff, meet your roommates, head off to the dining halls and campfires, and join the informal jams and classes, you'll feel the rush. You've made a couple of friends and started seeing familiar faces. The workshops take over. You're in a sleep-away, banjo theme park!

Typically, at a weekend or week-long banjo camp, you get intensive workshops, plenty of time to hang out with other campers, take part in jams throughout the day and often through the night, eat reasonable grub, and enjoy modest (but clean) lodgings. You also get a chance to collar, say, Tony Trischka, and have him sign the CD you just bought, or sit on the porch with Bob Carlin and get some help with a clawhammer lick you're trying to learn.

In spite of the perks and sheer fun of banjo camp, some folks find lots of good reasons not to go: mosquitoes, mud, loss of privacy, expense, time off from work, and travel hassles. That's why this book, with an entire banjo camp crammed inside, may be a better option than boarding the dog, stopping the mail, and driving a couple hundred miles to camp, thereby contributing to global warming and the coffers of a distant sheik.

What Is This Book Anyway?

Think of it as banjo camp between two paper covers, with its own soundtrack in the back. Like the real thing, *Banjo Camp!* is a combination of classroom instruction, unscheduled and friendly jam sessions, valuable tips and advice from the experts, and plenty of tall tales and banjo wisdom shared around the campfire.

To keep the action moving, we created a virtual camp we call Blue Mountain Banjo Camp (BMBC), run by an invented camp director, Buddy McCoy, who you'll hear from now and then. BMBC is a composite of several very real camps, festival workshops, and college-based programs.

We've situated the camp in the Blue Ridge Mountains of the Appalachian Range, an area that is the cradle of bluegrass and old-time music. Today, this music is no longer regional. Banjo camps and summer immersion sessions are located all over the United States—from Florida to New England and New York to California and Washington, with lots of points in between—plus Europe, Australia, and Japan. While there is no official census—organizing banjo pickers would be like herding cats—you'll find a listing of most major banjo programs at our website, www.banjocamp.us.

HERE'S WHAT YOUR CAMP EXPERIENCE INCLUDES:

- Slide show tours of several of the country's leading banjo camps

- Beginner's class in both bluegrass and old-time banjo taught by masters of the five-string banjo

- Interviews, workshops, and campfire conversations with (in alphabetical order) Bob Altschuler, Bobby Anderson, Bob Carlin, Janet Davis, Wayne Erbsen, John Herrmann, Geoff Hohwald, David Holt, Adam Hurt, Steve Kaufman, Bill Keith, Brad Leftwich, James McKinney, Alan Munde, Ken Perlman, Pete Seeger, Rich Stillman, Tony Trischka, Pete Wernick, and Todd Wright—and more!

- Slide show and lecture on the history of the banjo and banjo camps

- CD containing instruction and songs from the book, plus a play-along jam session to help you sharpen your new banjo skills

- Resource guide to real banjo camps and Internet sites, including www.banjocamp.us, where you can buy a new or used banjo, banjo supplies, a BMBC T-shirt, and meet fellow campers

BMBC is rewarding whether you're a complete beginner or someone with experience looking to ramp up his or her skills. Between these covers, you've got a full-blown beginning program in both bluegrass and old-time banjo, with advanced workshops by banjo Super-Heroes, many still wearing their capes and boots. Some of the most solid banjo players and teachers in the world are right here, on call day or night, whenever the banjo urge hits you.

 Pop in the CD and you can play clawhammer along with David Holt, or jam with Bobby and the Bluegrass Tradition right in your own home.

Sorry, no breakfast, but there's also no traffic, carbon emissions, gasoline bills and—best of all—you get to eat whatever you want and sleep in your own bed.

TIME FOR A BANJO

When you're ready to get down to the essential business of BMBC, you'll need a banjo. Or a friend with a banjo. Or a stiff piece of cardboard you can cut out to look like a banjo. However you "play" it, the idea is to have fun at Blue Mountain Banjo Camp. This approach to learning helped me along the way—and I bet this book…I mean…camp…can do the same for you.

Welcome Assembly

with Camp Director BUDDY McCOY

Welcome to Blue Mountain Banjo Camp. I'm Buddy McCoy, your camp director, a composite of real-life camp directors who will remain nameless. Any resemblance between me and any flesh-and-blood, banjo-picking, manual-writing, big-mouth, tone-deaf camp director living or dead is purely coincidental.

Sometime this afternoon, please come by the administration office (the white building on Piney Ridge) to pick up your nametag and lanyard, map, and schedule. While there, you can get directions to the Help Desk for answers to any of your questions. The schedule is critical to help you plan your workshops.

Meals are included. Of course we have a vegetarian option: *don't* pick up the meat-like substance at the buffet, and *do* take extra salad.

About lodging: We're fully booked, but if you find an empty bed, you're welcome to change your accommodations. Just notify your counselor so there's no ruckus at bed check. There are also motels in the village, next to coffee shops that serve very expensive lattes.

Tomorrow morning, after breakfast, we're assembling on the square outside the dining hall to bus on down to Asheville, North Carolina, for the Banjo Camp tour. You'll have the option to board the Bluegrass Express and watch a slide show of bluegrass banjo camps (we barrel through the Smoky Mountains and up north to New England), or climb into an open carriage for the Old-Time Horse & Buggy Tour of old-time banjo camps, which clops around the North Carolina foothills and the Piedmont, picking up hitch-hiking, clawhammer banjoists

en route to a few major events in the area. On each tour, you'll meet all the teachers leading workshops at Blue Mountain Banjo Camp this session.

If you're the impatient type, you can skip the tours and jump right into workshops in either the bluegrass or old-time track. In his workshop, Bobby Anderson covers all the banjo basics any beginner might need, before heading off into the mind-bending rolls and slides that make up a decent bluegrass version of "Cripple Creek." Frankly, I urge all you novices, regardless of your interest in old-time music, folk, or bluegrass, to take part in the first section of Bobby's workshop. You'll thank me later. After that, you'll be ready to participate in three monster bluegrass workshops taught by Alan Munde, Rich Stillman, and Bob Altschuler.

A highlight of old-time banjo instruction is the Music Hall Opera House production of "Georgia Buck Is Dead," starring David Holt. Then, check out Ken Perlman's workshop: he takes you from the pre-beginnings of clawhammer, stepping you through some solid air banjo before passing along the deepest secrets of frailing. Once you've got your bum-diddy down, Bob Carlin will demonstrate some of the century-old minstrel licks you can adapt to your own playing.

As part of your learning experience, head on down nightly to the Foggy Bottom meadow, where you can hang out with Pete Seeger, Tony Trischka, Janet Davis, Bill Keith, Brad Leftwich, John Herrmann, and Wayne Erbsen around the campfire.

If you're unlucky enough to require medical attention while at camp, dial 9-1-1, go up to the chapel, and wait quietly. Do not make a scene: banjo players are at work.

So, if you're ready, it's time to become an official banjo camper! Have fun! Banjo isn't something you learn—it's something you play.

Buddy McCoy

THE
Schedule

THE
Anatomy
OF THE Banjo

Consider it, this simple thing.

Round at the bottom, a long neck attached. Not at all shapely like a guitar or fiddle, nothing to fall into the curve of a human body. A child's toy.

So basic. A gourd, a pot, a drum with a stick attached to it. Just that, and strings made of gut or steel or anything at all, stretched from head to toe, from peg to tailpiece, to vibrate across the drum. That's all the banjo is. You can add a little bridge on the drumhead to the strings, and carry their vibrations to the pot. And tuning pegs to tighten the strings and change their tones.

In the banjo's basic tuning, there are only three tones. And although the neck is often long, there are only 12 frets before the sequence of notes and intervals repeats. Three tones, 12 frets, and only three fingering positions to sound all the major chords anyplace, up and down the neck.

But just when you think you've got the sober mathematical order of the five-string banjo down, you stumble over its true genius. The lunacy of the fifth string.

Shorter than the rest, its own tuning peg sticks out of the neck like an exclamation point, as if announcing its singularity.

There are four-string banjos with a venerable history in women's bands and Dixieland orchestras, traditional instruments used in some string bands and in New Orleans jazz ensembles.

But it's the fifth string that gives the thumb center stage in developing the sharp syncopated rhythm of the banjo, forever marking the banjo with its jingle jangle beat. That crazy fifth string creates the driving drone that reaches to the heart of the human soul.

This Appalachian, African-European mulatto child shares its gifts with ragtime, blues, folk, jazz, and classical musicians. In some hands you can hear minstrel and folk music bounce off the banjo, in some hands Bach, Gershwin, or Earl Scruggs.

Take it in your hands and start making some music of your own.

It's your ticket to banjo camp.

THE
Asheville
Trailhead
SLIDE-SHOW TOUR

Good morning.

There are three slide-show tours at Blue Mountain Banjo Camp. Starting things off is a quick look at Asheville, North Carolina, a small city with big ties to banjo.

If you're taking the Bluegrass Track, you'll be going to the rail station to board the Bluegrass Express (page 20). You'll be heading down south, then over the Smoky Mountains into Tennessee, and on up to New England before returning here for the Shindig the Village Green.

If you're on the Old-Time track, you haven't got far to go (page 68). We rigged up a Horse & Buggy Tour that will take you over to Madison County, up north a few miles, and then over to the Swannanoa Gathering out on the edge of town, and finally back for the Shindig.

Of course, since this banjo camp lives between the covers of your book, you can jump on and off either tour at will and switch around to your heart's content. Either way, we're starting out from Asheville.

Could we have the first slides, please?

Asheville, Downtown

Asheville, North Carolina, is changing, at a clip that will pretty much guarantee its old-time mountain culture will continue to erode like the mountains on which condos and gated communities are daily rising. So, if you want your friends to see a good part of the town Thomas Wolfe couldn't wait to leave, they better make plans to come on over before too long.

So what difference does it really make if another pretty little bed-and-breakfast southern town becomes the kickback getaway for the golf-link boomers?

It might make a difference to an endangered species— traditional banjo music.

A kissin' cousin to southern centers of bluegrass and old-time music, Asheville has played a special role in the evolution of American banjo.

In front of Asheville's downtown civic auditorium, there is a statue of a banjo player. The banjo has played an extraordinary role in preserving and fostering folk and country music in all its forms. The statue is a fitting, but small enough, tribute to the instrument that brought so much glory to this town. Why Asheville of all places?

The river must have something to do with it.

Wedged against the Blue Ridge Mountains at the eastern edge of the Appalachian Range's Great Smokies, Asheville was the cul-de-sac of the westward drift for early settlers headed out of the Piedmont. Later, fiercely independent settlers from Europe and immigrants from the Northeast would push on individually, carving out homesteads in the mountains, bringing provisions and supplies by horse and mule. To them, and their rude fiddles, banjos, and homemade instruments, we owe the preservation and creation of much traditional music. In the absence of roads and rails, development of mountain towns to the west and north of Asheville was limited.

The French Broad River, the third oldest river on Earth, and one of the few north-flowing rivers in America, circles around Asheville to the west and heads up into Tennessee. Until railroads finally breached the Smoky Mountains, the French Broad was a major traffic artery for goods from the Deep South. The river also brought wealthy plantation owners up from South Carolina and Georgia to spend their summers in the Blue Ridge Mountain air. They brought with them their retinue of African slaves, as well as a touch of wealth and support for the arts, all of which helped mold this southern Appalachian capital.

One reason for the association of Asheville with traditional music is a man by the name of Bascom Lamar Lunsford.

Bascom Lamar Lunsford

Born in Mars Hill, a few miles north of Asheville, Lunsford, a banjo picker, was a mountain musician who collected the songs and dances of Appalachia with passionate zeal. In 1927, he started a small music and dance event that celebrated its eightieth birthday in 2007. The Mountain Dance and Music Festival is the oldest continuous folk and music festival in the United States.

Bill Monroe

"It ain't bluegrass until the banjo starts playing," isn't far from the truth, ever since Earl Scruggs stepped on the stage of the Grand Ole Opry as a Blue Grass Boy in 1945 and unleashed a volley of staccato rolls that parted America's hair. But, bluegrass music, whatever its multiple origins, owes its name and beginnings to a mandolin player from Rosine, Kentucky—Bill Monroe.

The first appearance of the band, Bill Monroe and the Blue Grass Boys, was in Asheville. In the heart of a record cold winter, in a world swept by war and the unrelenting Great Depression, on February 2, 1939, at 3:30 p.m. on WWNC-AM in Asheville, a new group was presented on *Mountain Music Time*. Bill Monroe, mandolin; Cleo Davis, guitar; Art Wooten, fiddle; and comedian/jug player Tommy Millard were introduced as Bill Monroe and the Blue Grass Boys.

You can hear some of this history live. Wayne Erbsen, a musician, author, and academic based here in Asheville, posted a rich archive of music and interviews online at the Digital Library of Appalachia. When you get home, back to your computers, if you head on over to www.aca-dla.org, you can hear Cleo Davis tell the story himself.

America's oldest traditional music festival is in Asheville, and the debut of Bill Monroe and the Blue Grass Boys took place just a few steps from where we're standing right now at Pack Square. In the words of Bobby Fulcher, co-founder of the Tennessee Banjo Institute, the first banjo camp, "Western North Carolina was the primordial ocean out of which bluegrass-banjo style crawled onto sunlit shores. The evidence of co-evolution, cross pollination, and, yes, creation is abundant."

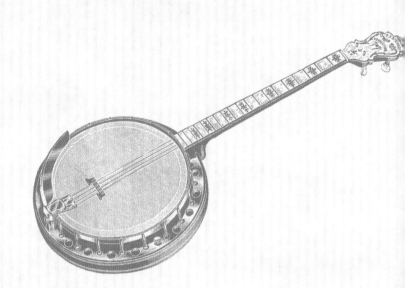

But, what about the most famous bum-diddy of all, the guy whose name is synonymous with the five-string banjo?

◀ Pete Seeger

Pete Seeger's father was an ethnomusicologist, his mother a violinist. "My mother bought fiddles for my older brothers," said Seeger. "When I came along, my father said, 'Let Peter enjoy himself.' He was curious to see what I would do…I first saw the five-string banjo played in 1936 in Asheville at the baseball park. There were 2000 people at Bascom Lunsford's Mountain Dance and Song Festival."

After that, the whole world saw what Peter would do.

◀ Earl Scruggs

The shadow of Earl Scruggs falls over every bluegrass banjo picker and the whole canon of bluegrass music. He created the sound that defines much of bluegrass today. Scruggs, from Shelby and Flint Hill, North Carolina, lived for a time in Hickory, just down the road a bit from Asheville.

Don Reno, who took over the banjo chores when Scruggs left Bill Monroe, lived in Clyde, the next town over. Frank Proffitt, banjoist and old-time fretless banjo builder, lived and performed in Asheville, as did Fiddlin' Bill Hensley, Aunt Samantha Bumgarner, and just a long list of good people.

So now that you have some idea of where we are, let's get on with the tour. As we ride along, you'll hear my stories about my own experiences at each of these banjo camps. I spent several weeks on the road, interviewing folks, making friends, learning new songs and licks. I didn't worry about the work and chores awaiting me back home, remembering John Hartford's dictum: "A banjo will get you through times of no money, but money won't get you through a time of no banjos."

Music, good times, dancing, community, and a lifting of the heart come through the doo-wop beat and high country voice of a five-string banjo. Hopefully, this quick tour through banjo camps will help spread some of that around in your direction.

All aboard. For the Bluegrass Express, just follow the signs to the station. Horse & Buggy Tour—y'all stay right where you are. I can hear your ride coming up the street now.

THE Bluegrass Express SLIDE TOUR — NEXT PAGE

THE Old-Time HORSE & BUGGY SLIDE TOUR — PAGE 68

THE Bluegrass Express SLIDE TOUR

This tour will chug on down the Nantahala Range to Cherokee County where Georgia, Tennessee, and North Carolina come together. We're visiting the John C. Campbell Folk School. Then we're headed over the Blue Ridge Mountains into Tennessee to stop at the Smoky Mountain Banjo Academy, then over to the North Carolina Piedmont for a look at Pete Wernick's Jam Camp. After a long haul up I-81, past the Virginias and Appomattox, we'll arrive in Groton, Massachusetts, a leafy suburb of Boston, for Banjo Camp North. Finally we'll wind up at Steve Kaufman's Acoustic Kamp in Maryville, Tennessee.

John C. Campbell Folk School

The total beginner who wants a taste of banjo might well consider the venerable John C. Campbell Folk School, deep in the woods of Cherokee County, in Brasstown, North Carolina. Depending on the workshop you select, you can find either low-key or high-intensity instruction in a small class environment. The Folk School, although not known as a banjo camp center, has a long history in mountain music, including the sponsorship of a women's banjo band early last century! Today, Folk School director Jan Davidson—between administrative chores—plays a fretless banjo, and banjo-picking ethnomusicologist David Brose directs the on-site museum and folklore program.

The campus, made up of barns, workshops, and rustic buildings dotted around the hilly landscape, is definitely rural. The staff and participants in various programs are creative, laid back, and friendly.

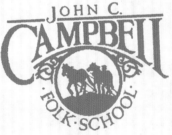

John C. Campbell Folk School is not your typical banjo camp. An argument could be made that it is not a banjo camp at all. Based on the model of the Danish collaborative, cooperative *folkehofjskole* or Danish Folk School, the John C. Campbell Folk School was launched with the donations and volunteer labor of 200 residents in 1925. It is internationally famous for offering a broad curriculum of traditional folk crafts and such survival arts as blacksmithing, agriculture, and carpentry, all presented in a bucolic corner of the universe in a cooperative environment where participants live and learn, together.

One of the arts—or crafts—offered is beginning banjo, as well as a mountain banjo construction course. Banjo is taught as a five-day resident program. And, while it isn't strictly speaking a banjo camp, the Folk School has been in the residential banjo-teaching business longer than any other camp in existence today.

At the Folk School, people in and out of the banjo program happily share their excitement about their projects. The John C. Campbell environment is inspirational, and the food was the freshest and most carefully prepared to be found on the tour.

✻ TWO TEACHERS, ONE BANJO

J.D. Robinson, one of the banjo instructors, is personable, experienced, and skilled as a teacher and performer. A chief of the local volunteer fire department, J.D. punctuates his teaching with his country tall tales and animated descriptions of theory, scrawled on an easel or demonstrated on his banjo. Back in the day, he toured with Clyde Moody and regularly performs locally.

◀ J.D. Robinson

His beginning banjo class, normally a handful of students, has all the advantages of face-to-face interaction and some of the disadvantages as well. A small class with varying skills and aspiration levels is a challenge to the teacher. On this tour we're seeing a morning class, a short lecture on the Nashville numbering system, illustrated with a little picking and storytelling. J.D.'s handouts cover essential theory, supplemented by his emphasis on singing melody and demonstrations of basic rolls and licks. The class was interrupted by a fire emergency in town requiring J.D.'s services. Even though our tour was cut short, it was clear the class was sociable, informative, and not overly rigorous.

◀ Geoff Hohwald

The other beginning banjo class at the Folk School, taught by Geoff Hohwald, takes a different tack. Hohwald, the author of a best-selling series of banjo instruction books, is far from the stereotypical bluegrass banjo picker. He's a city-dwelling, entrepreneurial, former encyclopedia salesman, uniquely focused on the business of banjo instruction. Geoff Hohwald could be the Dr. Strangelove of the bluegrass music business. Brilliant, hard-working, concocting learning systems in his computer laboratory late at night, merging music, business and computer technology, Hohwald takes his banjo learning programs into the field to refine and test their impact

on students. In the process, he teaches bluegrass basics with extreme efficiency.

Geoff has attention deficit disorder, a learning disability that forces him to plan meetings, lessons, and even conversations like he was building a Lego structure, one logical piece snapping into another. It might be one key to his success.

Another is the way he weds his logical analysis of the steps necessary to learn to play bluegrass banjo to his strong banjo skills and knowledge of computer and graphic systems. I was about to see all this in action at his week-long beginning banjo class.

We met the evening before his class. Geoff was setting up in a room. As he laid out his student binders filled with lessons and CD's and adjusted his multiple monitors and laptop driven systems, he talked a bit about how it all came about.

Geoff's Approach

"What started all this," said Geoff, plugging in machines and organizing workstations as he talked, "was that a student of mine was moving out of town. He wanted a cassette tape of the songs I hadn't yet taught him, along with the music and text. A friend produced a fairly nice tape and sold it to me for $10. While I was at it, I made 15 other copies, and my other students bought it, and all of a sudden I made $150 without actually having to work. I took the $150, rewrote the book, printed 200 books, and took them into the music store I worked at."

Before it was over, Geoff would parlay that initial $10 visit into a company with annual sales over $2 million.

"The reason I was successful and these books are so good is I have a learning disability. The way this attention deficit works for me is simple. If you explain something to me and you leave a step out, I get lost. I mean, I don't even think I'm lost. In creating the book, I go through this process in my mind. When I get to the point where I understand it, then everybody can understand."

Geoff's strongest suit is providing a banjo player who is working alone with a set of graduated exercises, a pathway—in tab and DVD—that will help him develop as a musician competent to jam. The essence of

Hohwald's approach is the introduction of small speed increments on bluegrass rolls played to a metronome set for one beat per click.

"So once they can play a roll at 45 beats per minute on the metronome, they get to go up to 50. See, all this represents is what any piano teacher would do with a metronome. If someone will play with this for a week or so, all of sudden he now has the roll down and is ready to move on. One reason it works is that the player can relax because he's increasing speed slowly.

"Second thing is the one metronome click, a click for each eighth note in a roll. You start getting one with the click. You start understanding that the purpose is to be in perfect time, and you actually have the sensation that a musician has with the band because everything is in perfect sync."

It's now nearly 10:00 p.m. Geoff scoops up his stuff, including the banjo with the loose tuning peg he's been working on while we talked. "Gotta go pick up some washers at Wal-Mart. See you tomorrow morning."

Technology Meets Banjo

At the Folk School the next day, Geoff, working with seven students, most brand-new to banjo (and music), had them playing together, vamping, and making chord changes. Using his method and technology to the hilt, he set up work stations in corners of the room where individual students, organized by capabilities, could watch DVDs of him playing simple licks or chord changes on the TV monitor. Geoff dashed from student to student, fast-forwarding the DVD, checking the student's performance, offering advice, and then hurrying on to check on another group of students.

With another banjo camp scheduled to begin on the weekend, I left Geoff and his class, video monitors and banjos blazing, and headed the Bluegrass Express into Tennessee.

Next stop on the tour, Jack Hatfield's Smoky Mountain Banjo Academy, is a totally different experience. Not a computer in sight, for one thing.

Smoky Mountain Banjo Academy

Smoky Mountain Banjo Camp (SMBA) has a special place in the pantheon of banjo camps. Started in 2004, in addition to being one of the newest camps, it has its roots in the original banjo camp, the Tennessee Banjo Institute where Jack was on staff. He directed the bluegrass program for TBI's successor, the Maryland Banjo Academy, launched by publisher Nancy Nitchie.

Jack Hatfield ▶

Jack Hatfield is known mostly as the author of several banjo instruction manuals and a regular long-term column in every banjo player's hometown paper, the *Banjo Newsletter*. A native Tennessean, he's based in Pigeon Forge, where he performs locally and runs his online cyber store, Hatfield Music. Just a bit down the road in Gatlinburg is Smoky Mountain Banjo Academy.

SMBA, emphasizing bluegrass banjo, is also one of the smallest camps, with about 30 registered students and an enrollment that swells slightly during the day with local walk-ins, and fills up considerably for the evening concerts that draw a crowd. As a result of its small size, you get to mingle—as in share scrambled eggs, porch chairs, and passing conversation—with such bluegrass elders as Bill Keith.

Bill Keith ▶

Bill Keith is most famous for applying notes from fiddle tunes directly to the banjo, refining and advancing the melodic bluegrass banjo style so that it's now usually called "Keith style." Another claim to fame: He produced the original tabs for Earl Scruggs' banjo instruction book. At camp he was also a bit infamous for walking around with a cigarette hanging off the corner of his mouth and wearing a black T-shirt with bold white letters proclaiming: "Sex, Drugs and Flatt & Scruggs."

Playing with Banjo Heroes

SMBA was a little bit like a bluegrass playground. Eddie Adcock, star performer with both the Country Gentlemen, and Bill Monroe, and a couple of other original Blue Grass Boys, taught workshops, performed at concerts, and participated in porch jams. In addition, there were basic courses taught by mortals like the redoubtable Janet Davis, and Winfield's National Banjo Champion winner James McKinney, and an occasional old-time workshop taught by Ken Perlman.

But the thing that sets SMBA apart from other camps is the chance it gives plebian banjos pickers to just hang out with larger-than-life banjo heroes. If you're into banjo at all, you own some of their records and tabs. At camp, you get to listen to these folks up on stage, a few feet away, sit across from them in a small classroom, and talk about stuff over coffee in the dining room. Sitting in on a porch jam with Eddie Adcock, Bill Keith, or Butch Robins just doesn't happen every day of the week. These are the guys who invented this music—they were in the stretch limo with Bill Monroe.

Open jams are all over the place—on porches, in rooms, the cafeteria, the company store, stairwells—everywhere students and instructors play bluegrass the way you always knew it could be played. Flat out, loud, and cooking. And, you get to join in.

Eddie Adcock feels this way about banjo camps: ▶

"I've taught in a lot of different settings and personally I like the hotel-type setting best for two reasons—it's easier and quicker to take elevators and get around to workshops and meals, and there's generally not far to go to get anywhere. But other people do like other kinds of workshops or camp settings, and they find it helps them if they get away from anything that looks like their old, regular daily grind. For some people, being outdoors or in a rustic setting helps them clear their minds for learning. Just make sure it's warm enough!"

The emphasis at SMBA is on bluegrass, but with Ken Perlman offering beginning clawhammer workshops and individual master classes, there was a serious, if limited, old-time component as well.

The core of SMBA is made up of practical workshops, like Janet Davis's backup banjo sessions, interspersed with concerts, private lessons, and seminar-type meetings where the banjo professor has a five-string strapped on his back, and mixes lecture and music.

Overcrowding in classes is not a problem. Between the founders and the next generation of pickers and instructors, like banjo maker-musician Tom Nechville, Snuffy Smith, Janet Davis, Rick Sampson, and others, there is an amazing 3:1 student-faculty ratio! Even that number improves, since you can book a half-hour one-on-one session with any instructor as part of your camp enrollment. And then there are the wide-open jams, but it takes guts to join in when you're sitting around the table with the likes of instructor James McKinney.

◀ James McKinney

McKinney is an impassioned teacher who has elevated banjo study to a spiritual practice, complete with visualizations, stretching exercises, and long monastic hours on the instrument. Spiritual or physical, the result is a solid block of searing sound made up of multiple rolls, ferocious bass-rhythm lines, and fusion riffs executed at blazing speed across music that can sound like John Hardy meets Jimi Hendrix.

Held at a woodsy, reclusive lodge, decorated with wandering peacocks exercising their high shrieks at random, SMBA earns great grades across the board. Jack Hatfield keeps things moving at a good clip, the country food is plain and ample, and the sound of banjos and jams comes at you from every porch and classroom. If you're into bluegrass, you might think you had died and gone to Foggy Mountain heaven.

Pete Wernick's Jam Camp

Our next stop on the Bluegrass Express is Pete (Dr. Banjo) Wernick's Jam Camp in Boomer, North Carolina. This place is commonly known as the pre-Merlefest camp because Pete's campers prepare a song to perform for the massive audience that attends Doc Watson's annual festival held on the campus of nearby Wilkes College. Pete's camp is like a one-room schoolhouse for some serious learning. Instead of 15 or 16 teachers, Jam Camp has Pete. There are breaks for jamming and assistants on hand to sit in with various groups, but instruction is given centrally by Pete, banjo in hand, with his wife Joan seated at his side playing guitar accompaniment, raising her fingers on occasion to let the assembled group know which chord is coming up.

Pete also runs bluegrass banjo-only camps, notably in Boulder, Colorado, and an advanced bluegrass banjo week at the Augusta Heritage program in West Virginia. Although banjos predominate, participants at Jam Camp bring a gamut of bluegrass instruments—harmonica, stand-up bass, mandolin, guitar, and fiddle.

This camp was held for the first time at Herring Ridge, a new YMCA facility near Wilkes College. It's a spread-out campus, with a high-ceilinged central meeting hall that incorporates a kitchen and dining facility. Floor-to-ceiling windows all around look onto outbuildings, dorms, and camper tent sites in the surrounding fields. Herring Ridge is some considerable distance from the main road and ringed by hills and forest. Accommodations are clean and spare, a dormitory setup of maybe a dozen double-decker beds in a room. There are separate quarters for men and women, separate quarters for heavy and light sleepers, and you bring your own bedding and towel.

Overall, accommodations and the food service seemed set up more for a kids' camp or an army platoon in basic training than a jamming music camp. However, you don't come here for the bluegrass cruise or four-star hotel treatment. You come to learn how to jam from the guy who has built a small empire showing people how to do it.

Pete Wernick

Pete Wernick calls himself industrious. Good call, since he is almost a one-man industry, churning out books, tapes, CDs, and DVDs over the course of 30-plus years, while also performing, recording, and running his floating jam camps around the United States, as well as banjo camps in Boulder, Colorado.

His camp is pitched to the beginner, for the most part, although there are a surprising number of participants who show up year after year. More than 300 jam campers have their own, very active Yahoo! group and share photos, music experiences, and plans to get together at the next camp.

Over the course of the weekend, in informal breakout groups, his jam campers play a good number of bluegrass two- and three-chord standards, but this is not the place to come unprepared. You're expected to show up knowing your basic chord forms and be able to sing—that's right, sing—at least two songs.

You even get homework assignments before arriving at camp, lists of tunes you might want to learn, and suggestions of things to do to make your time in camp most productive. To back up his good advice, Pete sends you to his extensive website, www.drbanjo.com, where, among other things, you can pick up a list of 54 two-chord songs, bluegrass jamming points, and the "Top 106 Jam Favorites."

Dr. Jim Bova prescribes Dr. Pete's banjo camp:

"When you go to his jam camp," says Ohio physician Jim Bova, "it's very clear you are expected to sing one or two songs. The key to bluegrass is singing—not instrumental banjo playing. So when you're doing these jam camps, when you go off in your small group, somebody has to sing, somebody has to arrange the breaks, and finish the song. To do that you have to know the melody and words."

◀ Alan Shaw

For bluegrass banjo players, singing seems to be the great hang-up, but for Alan Shaw, a native New Zealander, who came to Pete's Jam Camp from Australia, the Cabin Stage at MerleFest—the final event at Jam Camp—changed things around.

"Jam Camp," says Alan Shaw, "confronts one with the immediate need to have a fairly large repertoire of standard pieces at one's fingertips (so to speak). And being able to sing along is always going to be my greatest hurdle. But I'm learning. I like the way someone is expected to take a lead, to call the key, explain any intricacies of structure, and pace the musical time/rhythm. Making this happen is one of the best lessons we could have taken away from Jam Camp."

Mostly, Pete Wernick gives his campers permission to jam, taking away all excuses. In a sociological pressure cooker, where every level of play is permitted, the gentle pressure is on to play together in a group, sing a song in public.

The Wernick Jam Camp Experience

Many of the most popular performing banjo players in the United States teach at camps or privately. What's rare about the Wernick Jam Camp is that the full teaching program is carried by a top-ranked banjo player who is dedicated to teaching. And Pete Wernick has been at it a long time; he started an adult-ed, week-long summer program as part of the Portland State University Haystack Program back in 1980! He thought through the process of learning banjo, from his days as a kid hustling tickets to the first Flatt & Scruggs Carnegie Hall appearance so he could see how Earl did it.

Bluegrass in 1962 was still a novelty in New York—and in most of the rest of the world for that matter—when Pete was picking up riffs down in Washington Square Park from guys like Eric Weissberg and Marshall Brickman of the Tarriers. That was before he hooked up with Tony Trischka and, together with some other 20-something musicians, launched Country Cooking, a traditional/experimental bluegrass group. The lead singer for that group was Nondi Leonard, now known as Joan Wernick, the very same woman playing backup guitar and signaling chord changes for her

husband at Jam Camp, and the lead singer with Pete's bluegrass/jazz fusion group, Flexigrass.

Pete Wernick tapped into one powerful motivating force that makes people turn to music—jamming (playing music spontaneously with other musicians). Bluegrass, by its very nature—trading licks, taking breaks, playing backup, telling simple stories—is a social and communal event, where musicians and the audience share the joy and driving beat of the music, and play off one another.

He took that basic motivation, looked at the obstacles new players had to face, and came up with a simple formula that makes jammers out of newbies: Create a supportive atmosphere where beginning bluegrass players can start playing songs together from the very beginning. That's the bare bones of Jam Camp. If it sounds like a lot of serious work, that's because you can't hear the music, and you can't see the folks in camp having the times of their lives.

At night, from Pete's cabin porch down the hill from the main house, you can hear the sounds of a student jam coming from the main house, the banjo driving the rhythm and reaching out over the other voices with its rolling plunk and twang. Thanks to those little on-neck electronic devices lit up like fireflies in the night, the group was in tune. It may not have been perfect, but it was definitely bluegrass, and everyone was having a blast. It's the way to remember Jam Camp.

Banjo Camp North

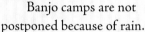

Banjo Camp North
May 18, 19, & 20, 2007
Groton, Massachusetts

Now it's time to put on your galoshes as we climb back on the Bluegrass Express and head up north.

Banjo camps are not postponed because of rain. So when it rained every day for the full Banjo Camp North session—a first in its five-year history—the festivities just stayed indoors. It's a tribute to the place and its director Mike Holmes that, after the first day, it just didn't seem to matter.

It was raining when I reached the gates of Banjo Camp North, actually a Baptist summer camp in Groton, Massachusetts. Deep muddy ruts led down to the Judson Cabins where I was bunked, which made driving treacherous and walking slippery.

Finding my room in the primitive cabin that had that summertime moldy smell familiar to campers everywhere was easy: I had a camp map in my welcome package. The ramshackle cabins were made up of a couple of rooms with bathrooms, a private room for an instructor, a shanty porch with a strong smell of wet wood and forest critters or whatever it is that lets you know you're not alone in this rain. My assigned bunk was wedged between two double-decker beds, across from a small bathroom. Even though I've been to other banjo camps, there are always some obstacles to negotiate. Snoring from neighboring bunks could be, to some, the toughest one, along with the distraction of nighttime bathroom runs and beams of flashlights. I needn't have worried. Sleeping, after a crammed day that starts around 7a.m. and continues on through late-night concerts and even later night jams, turned out to be no problem at all.

◀ Making Friends

I had two roommates, amiable guys, both from New England—one a young clawhammer banjo player, the other a bluegrass novice. We'd see each other at meals and concerts, crisscrossing campus on the way to classes. We had different workshop schedules, but we would exchange impressions at night and in the mornings. Roommates become a kind of family at camp.

Universally, everybody is friendly in camp. In that muddy, tightly scheduled, high-energy banjo environment, any other attitude would have been ridiculous. For three days and two nights, we played, ate, listened, and slept, surrounded by banjo music.

Mornings, campers hike up to classes and events. In the mud and rain, the old-time banjo campers had an advantage, since bluegrass banjos with their hard cases and tone rings weigh a lot more and were usually hand-carried around, while lighter-weight open-back banjos were generally strapped to the banjoists' backs.

It rained continually. Slogging through the mud with a banjo and a dripping camp schedule and map was part of the camp process. The dirt road leading down to the collection of sleeping cabins and up to the admin center was a slurry of mud and loose rock. Sometimes it was easier to drive to various buildings where classes and concerts were held, arriving at one of dozens of locations where ongoing seminars and workshops were being held.

The rain added a friendly sense of separation and isolation, as if it were an island instead of a Baptist bungalow colony a mile or so down the road from a pretty Massachusetts village. It also cemented solidarity among the campers, as we all faced the same smeary landscape on our way to a damp destination that would be ablaze with bright banjo sound.

BCN is big—more than 300 campers—and about equally divided between old-time and bluegrass banjo. Retirees predominate, but there were lots of boomers and young people as well, including kids young enough to need parents to sign consent forms. Women, while in the minority, were strongly represented in the old-time contingent.

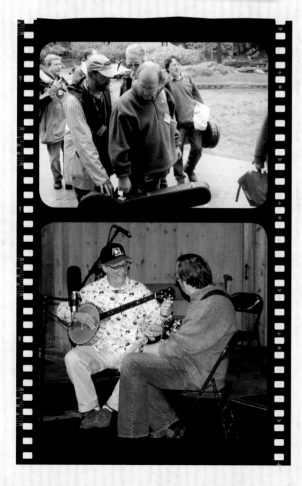

Star-Studded Teaching Staff

And then there was the teaching staff. All my classes were in the bluegrass track, so I got to study with Tony Trischka, Alan Munde, Bill Evans, Janet Davis (again), as well as guys I hadn't known before—New England-based Bob Altshuler and Rich Stillman—talented banjo pickers and terrific teachers and jam leaders who were patient and relentless working with students. Over mud treks and lunch, I did meet some of the old-time guys: Bob Carlin, Howie Bursen, Hank Sapoznik, and Brad Leftwich (pictured top left).

It was an excess of riches. I couldn't have known it then, but mountain roots music—rhythmic, syncopated, old-time clawhammer—would soon become important to me. That turn in the road, however, wouldn't really come for miles.

◀ Tony Trischka's "Double Banjo Bluegrass Spectacular"

Shortly before camp started, Tony Trischka's new CD was released, and along every parameter, it was stunning—a project that defined the current state of bluegrass banjo art. And here was Tony teaching a few classes along with another legendary performer, Alan Munde. Pretty much, I stayed on the bluegrass track, had a spectacularly great time, heard terrific music, laughed at dumb jokes, and got a good sense of what it's like to play in a high-octane bluegrass group. Like most participants, I took very little away in new material—a couple of new songs, a few licks, and lots of ideas about how to break down a song. Classes are about an hour and a quarter. The material comes fast and is accompanied by high-level banjo picking. Most of the time, I just kicked back, noodled a bit, and went along for the ride, figuring it would soak in sooner or later.

◀ Banjo Pit Stop

An unanticipated benefit of Banjo Camp North was the vendor area. Along with a rich assortment of tapes, CDs, and books, manufacturers displayed new banjos, handed out free strings, and were happy to share technical setup details.

Todd Wright, tech ambassador for Deering Banjo, manned his booth and backed up the Deering lifetime guarantee to the hilt. He took my used Sierra apart, slapped on a new bridge, reset the action, and then removed the resonator back so he could reposition the armrest in a more comfortable position. A photo call for all campers interrupted the process, so I headed off to the gym holding the banjo together under my arm.

Say Cheese

Ah, the photo shoot. Every camp does it, even the granddaddy of them all, Tennessee Banjo Institute. It's fun to see all the campers and staff together in one (dry) place. On the echoing gym floor, with folks arranged by size on stadium benches by the photographer, who looked a lot like my last vice principal, it evoked memories of high-school events. While there may be little real demand for the final product—a three-foot-long print of 300-odd banjo players—it's traditional and a break in the rhythm of a day given over, almost monastically, to banjo. Besides, it will look cool up on the camp's website.

Evening concerts at BCN, up in the chapel, were easily worth the price of admission to the camp itself. The best of old-time and bluegrass banjo players joined world-class fiddlers, bass players, mandolinists, and guitarists in a succession of performances that brought the audience out of their seats. It wasn't always polished, but it was high-energy, creative, and intimate music. Afterward, campers with umbrellas or rain gear filed down the wooded paths, picking their way with the help of flashlights and the slashing headlights of cars headed back to the cabins or to one of the several nighttime jam sites.

Sunday morning, the weather broke, intermittently. A black Harley-Davidson motorcycle, parked under a tree with its weatherproof banjo case attached to the side like a western stagecoach rifle sling, barely dried off before the rain started up again, slicking its black paint.

Theme Time

After breakfast I had to choose between Alan Munde's Bluegrass Banjo Tools and Techniques and Tony Trishka's Composition Workshop for the Banjo. Getting lost en route, I ended up in Judson Lodge, in Bill Evans's workshop, "Theme Time": Increasing Knowledge of Passing Chords. "Theme Time" was the one new song I learned in camp.

Bill Evans (pictured right), fresh from his final edits on his *Banjo for Dummies*, has an easy sense of humor and an intense teaching style. They work together well. He breaks down a song, works through each section, without tab, and then leads the group, measure by measure, into the tune.

In this case, "Theme Time" has a simple opening—really little more than a string of licks—followed by a dramatic Part B that ascends way up the neck in a series of disguised repetitions that lets you, in Bill's words, "sound better than you really are." After the session, he handed out the tablature for the piece.

"Here's something for you," Bill told the class, "to show back home when your friends ask you what songs you learned at banjo camp." Everybody laughed. With all the technical workouts and jamming, even though I felt crammed with new and exploding banjo knowledge, I hadn't learned a single piece. Later on, back home, breaking out Bill's tablature version of "Theme Time," I realized he had gotten it across without the printed page, and I could play it after all.

And now, just like Bill said, I can play a song and sound a lot better than I really am. Except there's this difference: The trick to sounding good was using those passing chords—small routines that lead from one chord to another. And thanks to this workshop, I had new ways to make that happen in everything I played from here on out.

That Sunday morning workshop was a highlight, but it was immediately followed by an even more powerful class—the workshop called The Twin and Triple Banjo Spectacular—led by three monster banjo players: Tony Trischka, Alan Munde, and Bill Evans.

The title of the class was a take-off on Tony Trischka's chart-busting CD, *Double Banjo Bluegrass Spectacular*, the bluegrass album featuring Tony in duet with Earl Scruggs, Bela Fleck, Alison Brown, Steve Martin, and others. Simply having these three master bluegrass banjo players appear together would be some kind of significant event, but due to a blister on her thumb, the scheduled bass player had to drop out. Standing in for her was Eric ("Dueling Banjos") Weissberg, the real banjo player in the movie *Deliverance*. They were backed up by Lincoln Meyers on guitar and Phil Zimmerman on mandolin.

Left to right: Phil Zimmerman, Tony Trishka, Alan Munde, Eric Weissberg, Bill Evans, Lincoln Meyers

◀ **Bruce Kriviskey, a banjo freshman, tells all:**

"This is my first camp. It's been a good immersion. I'm 68, and camp has been exhausting. But I started jamming, and I'm inspired. I'm ready to go home and practice, practice."

Steve Kaufman's Acoustic Kamp

At first, I had no plans to attend Steve Kaufman's Acoustic Kamp as part of this banjo camp tour. I wasn't even aware that SKAK—an award-winning guitar music camp—offered banjo instruction until I saw the flyer in a local music store. Since the camp was just a couple of hours over the mountain, I called Steve who invited me up to have a look.

SKAK isn't hard to find once you hit the small town of Maryville, Tennessee. Maryville College is at the center of the town and when I visited, the college campus had been taken over by Steve Kaufman's music camp. Even if you miss the banners and signs with the omnipresent SKAK logo, you see streams of musicians carrying instrument cases shuffling in and out of the college buildings between classes, and small groups jamming on the library steps, the concrete slabs near the cafeteria entrance, and the lawns.

Maryville College, the alma mater of Steve Kaufman's wife, camp co-director Donna Dixon, is one key to the enormous success of SKAK. With built-in dormitory rooms, classrooms, auditoriums, and institutional kitchen and dining facilities, the venue is perfectly suited for a music camp.

Originally a guitar camp and later a mandolin camp, you would think banjo was just an add-on to this event. It's not. SKAK offers beginning and intermediate banjo programs in both old-time and bluegrass styles, with serious teachers like Murphy Henry (as in, the "Murphy Method"), Eddie Collins, Pat Cloud, and Ross Nickerson on the bluegrass side, and Wayne Erbsen, Cathy Fink, and Laura Boosinger teaching old-time banjo.

◀️ Casey Henry

Waiting to hook up with Steve, I wandered around the campus. A slow jam was in progress—maybe 30 or 40 musicians, mostly guitars, one bass, and a sprinkling of mandolins, banjos, and Dobros. Murphy Henry's daughter, Casey, a Nashville bluegrass musician in her own right, has been teaching here for four years. She's focused on Beginner Level One and leads slow jams. Casey was calling out chord changes and singing as the jammers played. After the jam I asked her how it was going.

"Students really like it. It's a little hard yelling out chords first thing in the morning, but it's good. This year, we pick one song. We'll do that song all day. The afternoon jam is a little faster than the morning jam. In the slow jam, we do basic songs people know, do them slow, and play them for a long time so people can practice them. Many of the same people come through to the faster jam. Slow jams can be useful for people at any level. More advanced players can try out different chord positions or play up the neck."

Casey adds that it's mostly adults who come to camp—middle-aged people who have the resources and time off work. "A lot of people use it for their vacation. The people who teach here are really famous, world-renowned. Mostly this is a guitar camp. The banjo world is smaller."

There is an upside to this for banjoists. At banjo camps, a few ringers are brought in to make up a bluegrass band—bass players, guitarists, fiddlers, mandolins. Here, banjo pickers are in demand.

Two young women were sitting nearby on the grass, one playing banjo, the other mandolin. Kaleigh Malloy from UNCA, Greensboro, and Stephanie Friedman, from Boston University, went to high school together in Atlanta.

"We're both beginners," said Stephanie.

"Hard-core beginners," said Kaleigh. They both laughed. "We sing together all the time and thought we should play an instrument. My new year's resolution was to learn how to play the mandolin."

"My mom's here," said Stephanie, "I invited her along. She's in the old-time banjo program."

"So far in camp, we did scales, only G so far, and chords," said Kaleigh. "I can pick and read tablature, but I want to put a style underneath it—the trills or tremolos and the stop things. Casey Henry's teaching us one song a day. But we can sing."

They both started singing, very sweetly, to the slow strummed accompaniment of mandolin and banjo.

Take It Away, Steve!

Then Steve came out and we pulled away to talk a bit.
A record-breaking three-time winner of the flatpicking
Winfield (Kansas) nationals, Steve is prolific. He has
published more than 100 books and CDs, all distributed
by Mel Bay or HomeSpun, with two new books and nine
CDs ready for release. He has also built one of the largest,
fastest-growing music camps.

"We'll have 600 students over the course of the two-
week program and almost 100 family members who come
with the students. And we have 46 teachers for the two
weeks." Week one is given over to flatpicking, fingerpicking,
Dobro, bass, old-time banjo, and fiddle. Week two is
flatpicking, mandolin, and bluegrass banjo."

Even though SKAK built its reputation as a guitar
camp when it opened its doors in 1996, it has been adding
new instruments and styles ever since. About half the
campers play guitar and half play other string instruments. If it doesn't have the overwhelming breadth of
banjo instructors found in a pure banjo camp, the diversity
makes for terrific jamming opportunities.

There are bound to be growing pains in a music
camp that has expanded so rapidly and attracts students
from around the world. For example, putting the very
large beginning banjo class on stage in the auditorium, as
opposed to a classroom, poses line-of-sight problems for
both students and the instructor. It's a problem sure to be
corrected. The sole director and organizer Steve acts on
input from campers and faculty as part of his "build and
settle" development strategy.

Considering his prowess as a champion flatpicker, I
asked Steve if he had any practice tips to pass along to banjo
pickers. Not surprisingly, he had a system. You'll find it in
the camp library—or back of the book—called Homework.

Right now, we're just going to drop you off here at the
Blue Mountain Banjo Camp station. The Bluegrass Express
is headed back to our Asheville home base.

For those of you getting off this tour to start your
bluegrass workshops—and for all beginners looking for
a solid first step—it's time to tune up. Bobby Anderson's
Beginning Bluegrass Workshop is right over there on the
back porch by the creek.

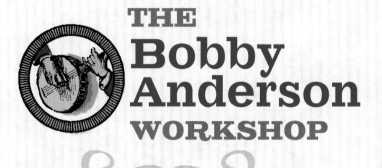

THE Bobby Anderson WORKSHOP

INTRODUCTION

Chances are you've never seen Bobby Anderson play. Even though he's been knocking around the back roads and interstates, performing at coffeehouses, bluegrass and folk festivals, and on concert stages for the past nearly 40 years, he's rarely the star performer. He did party with the Kingston Trio, share a bill with lots of headliners, and one snowy night in Fort Smith, Arkansas, his band opened for the Earl Scruggs Revue, but that's not typical of his career as a banjo player.

Bobby has a popular Western North Carolina group, Bobby and the Bluegrass Tradition, but you probably don't have one of their CDs in your collection. His recording projects are independently produced and distributed, and get airtime on local bluegrass and country music stations.

He may not be the fastest, most famous banjo player at this year's Blue Mountain Banjo Camp, but we're lucky to get him to head up our beginner's bluegrass track. Bobby is that back-porch pickin' uncle most of us were never lucky enough to have. He's patient, he's clear, he knows pretty much everything about playing bluegrass banjo, and he has an unlimited bag of songs and styles. And he is a born teacher. I know. He introduced me to real bluegrass picking.

Born in Tulsa, Oklahoma, Bobby picked up his early music education the usual way, singing at home and in church choirs. But instead of quitting at a reasonable age, he went on to work with a couple of high school buddies in an a cappella barbershop trio group called the StepTones until, one day, he heard the Kingston Trio. He wanted that instrumental backup for his group and for himself—that Dave Guard banjo sound.

☼ LEARNING THE BASICS

Bobby went to the local music store and asked the lady behind the counter for a banjo. "Would that be five string or four string?" she asked. "Just a minute, ma'am," he said, and went to the back of the store to look at the album covers. Sure enough, there was the Kingston Trio, and Dave was holding a five-string banjo.

"Heck, if they didn't have that album, I might be playing Dixieland on a tenor banjo today," Bobby said.

Back then Bobby was strumming his banjo, folk style, relying on Pete Seeger's classic *How to Play the Five-String Banjo*, until he ran across a world-class frailer, Steve Brainerd, in Oklahoma City. "I would drive down from Tulsa once a week, to sit in the front row at the Buddhi coffee shop just to watch him play. Steve could play banjo all different styles. It really opened my ears—country, folk, blues. You don't have to do fast frailing songs; you can make the banjo sound sweet. This instrument could be made to play anything you wanted to hear."

Soon, though, what Bobby most wanted to hear was bluegrass. "The guy that really started me playing bluegrass was Joel Burckhardt in Tulsa. This was 1966 and I had not started picking yet, and he would say, 'Do you know how to do this?' And we got together and he showed me the rolls so I could figure out how it worked."

"The sound of the banjo was always in my ears," Bobby remembers. "As kids we had to go to bed early, and we would listen in my bed to the Grand Ole Opry, and I couldn't tell if I was listening to Earl Scruggs or J.D. Crowe, but the banjo was the sound that struck me. Once Joel put me on to the roll and the use of the fingers, I got interested in how it worked. Joel Burckhardt was an engineer for Martin Marietta, never went professional, but he's one of the best pickers I ever met."

Blue Ridge Music
Asheville North Carolina

❊ BLUE RIDGE MUSIC CENTER

These days, it's Bobby showing folks the ropes as a fully booked banjo teacher in his own shop. In 2000, Bobby moved to Asheville, North Carolina, to be with his kids and new granddaughter. Bobby and his wife Susie bought a music store and renamed it the Blue Ridge Music Center. He started a weekly Monday night bluegrass jam that's been going on every Monday night, except holidays, for five years.

There's no charge. It's just Bobby paying back Dave Guard, Joel Burkhardt, Steve Brainerd, and that music store lady behind the counter 40 years ago. If you find yourself in Asheville, North Carolina, on any Monday evening, just come by the store, pull up a chair, if you can find one, tune up, and join in.

Right now, though, he's taking time off to teach some banjo fundamentals at Blue Mountain Banjo Camp. So have fun and listen up. Bobby, you're on.

LESSON: BEGINNING BLUEGRASS

Good morning. Let's take this from the very beginning. You get home from the music store with your new five-string banjo. Where do you start?

You might start by remembering the most basic thing of all: The banjo is an instrument to make music that will get folks moving and happy! And put yourself at the head of the line of those folks about to be made very happy. There is something about the sound and rhythm of the banjo that will just set your feet stomping and your face smiling.

If you're just starting out, you can get to that point a lot faster by taking a quick tour of your banjo and seeing what the parts are all about. The big round white plastic part is the banjo head. It's attached to the rim with adjustable hooks. The five strings run from the tailpiece through a wooden bridge sitting on the head, and continue on over the long fretboard up to the headstock, where they're attached to moveable tuning pegs...except for the fifth string that makes a detour to its home at a tuning peg right off the fifth fret. You'll be using those pegs to tighten the strings to their appropriate pitch.

When plucking or strumming the strings, the banjo sound primarily resonates off the bridge, the head, and the wooden rim.

The five-string banjo is unique in that the fifth string is an octave tone made to go with all the chords in the key to which the banjo is tuned. The most common tuning for a banjo is the key of G, where the open strings sound the G chord. In this tuning, the fifth string is tuned to a G note, the fourth string to a D; the third or middle string is also a G. The second string is tuned to a B, and the first string is a higher D note. Five strings but only three tones.

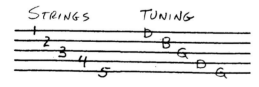

It's a good idea to use a banjo strap, if you have one, when you play the banjo. The strap distributes the weight more evenly and, when attached, will hold the neck up without you having to use your fingering hand to support the banjo.

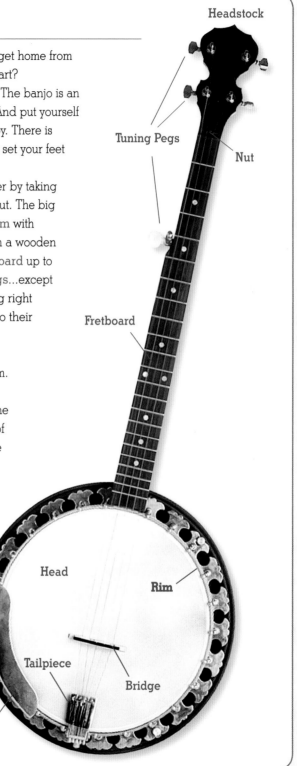

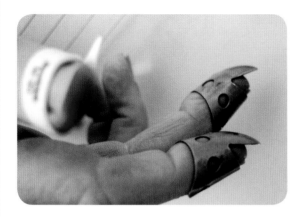

Put On Your Picks

Now it's time to put on your picks. Some people compare wearing fingerpicks to taking a shower with your socks on. But if you're going to play bluegrass, you might as well get the hang of it right off. Why abuse your fingers with picks? Sound! Try picking a string with a bare finger. Now put on a pick and pick the same string. You'll hear how the pick produces a much louder and clearer tone. Most banjo players use a plastic thumb pick, and metal finger picks covering the fleshy tip of the index and middle fingers. Try out a few different weights and types of fingerpicks. You can bend the ends to curve around your fingertips or let them stick straight out. It's picker's choice.

At the heart of bluegrass banjo is the *roll*, the steady rhythmic motion of the picking fingers playing continuous arpeggios, or chord tones. When organizing a roll pattern, make sure you're picking eight evenly spaced beats per measure.

When you start practicing rolls, forget about your left hand. Practice your rolls on open strings. Start SLOW. Speed is not important. Clarity and accurate timing are the critical musical elements you're acquiring through your practice. And once you have a toolbox full of bluegrass rolls, we'll go over some of the ways you can choose the roll that best picks out the melody notes of the song you're playing.

There's nothing boring about a five-string banjo. The sound can be soulful, stirring, and ear splitting. But never boring. How do those guys get so many notes out of five strings with only three fingers? It's not really magic.

The secret is learning to pick with one hand while fingering notes with the other.

Getting Familiar with Tabs

First, let's look at a tablature sheet: five lines representing the five strings of your banjo. The line on top is the 1st string…the bottom line is your 5th string (the shorter one). If there is an "0" written on (or sometimes above) a line, you play that string open or unfretted. If there is a number on the line, like a "2" on line four, you press down the 4th string just behind the 2nd fret for optimal clarity.

```
O = OPEN STRING    NUMBER = FRET COVERED
```

Tablature or tab gives you the proper chord or melody note to create music. Now let's examine the roll. A roll requires you to use your "picking" hand (usually the right hand) in an organized manner in order to pluck eight beats per measure. Let's start with two of the most common rolls, the *alternating thumb roll* and the *forward roll*. When practicing rolls, use only the picking hand and play all strings open.

THE ALTERNATING THUMB ROLL

The first roll is the alternating thumb roll. Start by plucking the 3rd string with the thumb (a G note), and then pluck the 2nd string with your index finger (a B note). Now pluck the 5th string with the thumb (another G note), and then the 1st string with the middle finger (a D note). We're halfway through: now repeat what you just did—thumb on the 3rd string, index on the 2nd, thumb on the 5th string, and middle finger on the 1st string. This pattern is written as T-I-T-M. All the notes should have the same timing or beat; it's what gives you the metronome effect for everyone to follow. You can see how it looks in tab at the bottom of the page.

If you pop in your CD and go to Track 10, you'll hear me play this alternating thumb roll.

POP IN YOUR CD NOW

Tracks 8 & 9:
Tune up your banjo with Bobby.

THE FORWARD ROLL

The next basic roll is the forward roll. This roll is unique because the picking hand always goes in the same direction. You will pick thumb, index, middle, thumb, index, middle, thumb, index, middle, and start again. It's very important that you stop and start again to keep the eight-beat-per-measure time intact.

A typical forward roll of eight notes could go like this: Thumb (3rd string), index (2nd string), middle (1st string), thumb (5th string), index (2nd string), middle (1st string), thumb (3rd string), and index (2nd string). Here these rolls are written in tab.

Again, listen to the CD to hear how this sounds (Track 11).

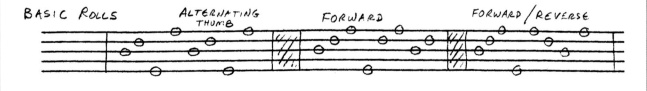

BASIC ROLLS   ALTERNATING THUMB   FORWARD   FORWARD/REVERSE

THE DOUBLE THUMB ROLL

Another technique you'll use is called *double thumb*. When there is a melody note every other note, a complete roll isn't possible. We then will pluck the melody note with the thumb and a backup note with a finger. For example, pluck the 4th string, open, with the thumb, then the 2nd string open, with the index finger, then the 4th string, fretted at the 2nd fret, with the thumb and continue on as shown in the tab.

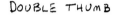

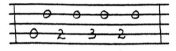

THE SLIDE

Let's look at and listen to a fingering hand technique called the *slide*. Sliding involves covering a string at one fret and sliding your finger to another fret on the same string while holding the string down. The string held down on the fretboard is essential for a clean, smooth slide. Feel those "speed bumps" as you cross each fret and you're doing it right.

To prepare yourself to play most bluegrass songs on your banjo, you need two things. You must first be able to roll these rolls accurately and easily, and then you need to know the three basic chords in the key of G: G-C-D7.

CHORDS

Right now, let's handle the basics of forming chords to get you started.

A chord is three or more notes played together harmonically. This is called a *triad*. On your banjo, strumming the strings open or unfretted gives you the three notes of a G chord or triad. These notes are G (3rd and 5th strings), B (2nd string), and D (1st and 4th strings). When you fret any of these strings, you change the tone of that string. Most songs have more than one chord in them to make up a melody.

The basic chords for the key of G are G-C-D, also shown on the example sheets. The G chord is open on all strings. To make a C chord, use the ring finger to fret the 1st string at the 2nd fret, the index finger to cover the 2nd string at the 1st fret, and the middle finger to cover the 4th string at the 2nd fret. Leave the 3rd string open. (Look at the diagram for the C chord that shows the finger positions at the string and fret.) Now strum all the strings for a C chord.

Look at the diagram for the D7 chord and fret the strings as indicated, When you think you have it, strum across all strings to hear a D7 chord. If it sounds awful, you either aren't fretting the string at the right fret, or you aren't holding your finger down on the string close to the fret, firmly. Try again, you'll get it.

Notice how similar the C and D7 chords are? In switching from C to D7, all you really have to do is leave your index finger in place, and switch fingers on the 2nd fret, from your ring finger on the 1st string, to your middle finger on the 3rd string. You can hear me play the G, C, and D7 chords, on Track 8.

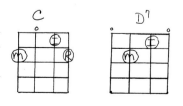

Once you can make both the C and D7 chords easily and are able to use both the forward roll and alternating thumb roll, you're ready to start playing some music.

Advanced Beginner Level

We're going to play a bluegrass standard, something most folks in a bluegrass jam know. It's called "Cripple Creek."

First, pop in your CD to Track 13 and listen to me and the band play the song.

Nice, huh?

Okay, now take a look at the tab sheet for the song. How many roll patterns can you find? A song in standard 4/4 time like "Cripple Creek" has eight beats in each measure. Yeah, you noticed, didn't you? Not all of these measures have eight notes. But they all have eight beats. When you see an "X" behind a note, that means a pause for one beat, the time it would take you to play an eighth note.

When you see two notes written directly under one another, that means you will play them at the same time, or "pinch" them together. Now that makes a little more sense, right? All the eighth notes in a measure have a little flag attached to their mast. Quarter notes, which are counted as two eighth notes, have no flag.

So here's a pop quiz. How many quarter notes in an eight-beat-measure?

If you said four, you're ready to pick, but chances are you'll find precious few notes in a bluegrass song that aren't eighth notes or their speedy relatives, the 16th note (identified by having two flags flying from its mast).

Following the melody the first measure of the "Cripple Creek" arrangement starts with a pinch of the 1st and 5th strings, with the 1st string fretted at the 2nd fret. You then slide up the 1st string to the 5th fret. This is a long slide that takes two beats. Then play the 5th string open, followed by a one-beat pause. Next, pluck the 1st string open with a pause (two more beats), and finally pluck the 2nd string open with a pause (two more beats), totaling eight in all.

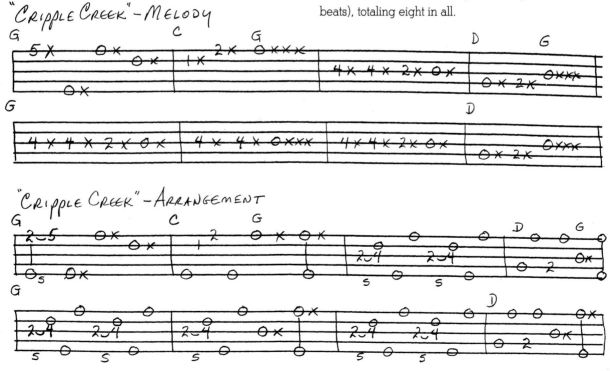

Now check out your tab sheet again. See how much clearer it is than describing the placement and movement of your fingers on the frets and strings? All you have to do is look at the map of the banjo fretboard on the tab sheet and you have a diagram of the entire process. As you become familiar with your banjo, you'll be able to rely more and more on picking out songs by sound, but tablature is always a useful, quick way to build up your song skills and inventory.

Ready to try working out the second measure before reading on? Pick up your banjo and see if you can figure out how the tablature translates to your fretboard. Once you get the hang of it, it's a natural way to learn music and one of the first music notation systems ever used.

Notice that the second measure is split in that two different chords are played within the eight beats. First, make your C chord, and then move on to the open 5th string. Next, play your G chord by plucking the 1st string open, and then pause and pinch the 1st and 5th strings, both open. Do you see how the tab says all that? Good!

In the third measure, you'll be using the alternating thumb roll for timing and adding a slide from the 2nd to the 4th fret on the 3rd string. The roll rhythm is the most important part of this measure, so make sure the slide is within the roll itself.

Here's how:

Pluck the 3rd string, covered at the 2nd fret, with the thumb, and while the string is vibrating, slide up to the 4th fret. Notice how the slide will reach the 4th fret about the same time as the index finger is plucking the 2nd string, open. Then pluck the 5th string, open, and the 1st string, open, and you're halfway there. Repeat the roll with the slide for another eight beats.

Even though you're aiming for the fast, crisp, and wild banjo sound, you're not there yet. Go slow. Go very, very slow. It's important that you play precisely and rhythmically, and the only way to do that is to play very slow. We'll start building up speed later on, but if you start practicing your mistakes now, then later on you'll just be playing very fast mistakes.

I'm going to let you figure out the next part of "Cripple Creek" on your own, using the tab sheet. The chords and all finger positions are marked, so if you take it slow you should have no problem putting it together. Track 14 on the CD features a nice, slow version of the song, followed by a regular version (Track 15). Once you work it out on your own, check the CD to see how you're doing.

Got it? Well done! "Cripple Creek" is your first song. In order to play it, you had to learn to read a tab sheet, make two chords, and play a song using a slide and two rolls. But before breaking your picking arm patting yourself on the back, practice "Cripple Creek" dozens of times a day until you know it by heart and can play it without missing a beat! That's the secret of bluegrass banjo. Play without any gaps or holes. Work on your timing until all notes and pauses in "Cripple Creek" have the same beat. Timing for a bluegrass banjo picker is more important than speed or "hot" licks. You are the metronome for the band and the jam session. Without solid timing from you, the music will fall apart.

POP IN YOUR CD NOW

Tracks 15 & 16:
"Cripple Creek"

Most of what you will do when you play is back up other folks. Backup is the foundation the song is built on. Each instrument in a band has a unique contribution to the backup role, something we'll cover later on. Right now, let's look at the banjo roll as a backup tool.

Backup Banjo

When you're using an eight beat roll, you're providing the basis for the melody to be sung or played by another instrument while you hold the timing solid. Let's examine a backup for "Cripple Creek" using our two basic rolls.

"Cripple Creek" has two parts—a verse and a chorus. The verse has four measures: The first measure is a G, the second is split between the C and C, the third measure is G again, and the fourth measure is half D and half G.

✹ MEASURE ONE

For measure one (see the tab) we'll use the forward/reverse roll, T-I-M-T-M-I-T-I. Play this measure on open strings.

✹ MEASURE TWO

In measure two we'll switch to the alternating thumb roll (T-I-T-M), first in C and then in G. If you forgot the chord positions, just check the chord charts or look at the fingering on the tab sheet. See how perfectly the alternating thumb roll works with a split measure?

✹ MEASURE THREE

Since the third measure is a G, we'll return to the forward/reverse roll, and for the fourth measure, also a split, we'll use the alternating thumb roll again.

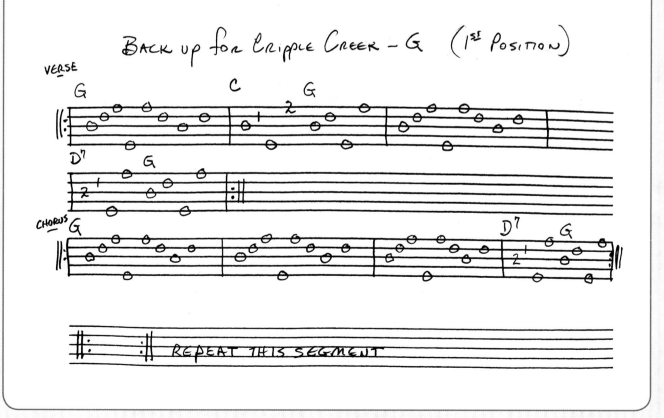

The chorus backup can be played by using the forward/reverse roll, starting with the thumb on the 3rd string. Play this three times for G, and then try switching to the alternating thumb where the tab sheet calls for the D7.

Taking these tips and the tab sheet, work out the lead and backup versions of "Cripple Creek"—SLOW—and practice your rolls and slides so they come together like clockwork timing. Use a metronome if you can and record yourself. Recording is a good way to isolate areas that need work. Once you have it together, pop in the CD and play along with the slow version of "Cripple Creek" first. When you're ready, jump into the jam, which gives you the opportunity to play both solo and backup, and get the feeling of playing with a group of musicians.

With practice you can now play lead or melody, and back up others who are playing lead or singing. If you take this approach with all your songs—whether you download them from the Internet, or learn them from books or friends—you'll be a welcome addition to any jam session.

Intermediate Level

"John Hardy" is an intermediate song in that it uses all three left-hand techniques: hammer-on, pull-off, and slide. You developed your slide in "Cripple Creek," so let's look at the hammer-on.

❖ HAMMER-ON

Hammering-on is a technique common to most string instruments. You pluck a string and drop your finger forcefully on the vibrating string above the fret that is sounded. For example, if you're fingering the 2nd fret on the 1st string with your index finger, you would pluck the string and then strike down on the 3rd fret with your middle finger. It's not necessary to apply a great deal of force since all you're doing is raising the pitch of the note by fretting at a higher point.

✹ PULLING-OFF

Pulling-off is a related, but opposite technique. In this case you already have a string fretted, say the 4th string at the 2nd fret. When you pluck the string, you sound a note and then pull your finger off the string, snapping the finger against the fingerboard. The snap has to be hard enough to sound the note at a volume equal to the preceding fretted note. To do this you can either push off (up) or pull off (down) on the string.

For example If you're fretting the 4th string at the 2nd fret with your middle finger, you can pull off to an open string or you can have your index finger placed on the 1st fret, so the pull-off is lowered by a half-tone. Pull-offs are very useful to add speed to cascading runs. Both hammer-on and pull-off techniques are essential parts of bluegrass.

Several different rolls can be used to get the melody out of a song. In "John Hardy," these are shown on the tab sheet. Remember, an "x" equals a one-eighth-note pause, so count it silently to keep the timing true. When two notes are written directly underneath one another, pinch them together. The slide, hammer, and pull off must be played within the tempo of the roll itself.

Now it's time to really have fun with your banjo. You can play melody by picking out the notes and adjusting your roll, and you can play dynamite backup to any song by just rolling consistently.

Work with the practice roll tabs, and take "John Hardy" apart just the way we did "Cripple Creek." After you've practiced a while, check out "John Hardy" on the CD, Track 19. Then go to Track 20: the boys and me are playing it and we've left a chair for you.

And, did I say practice slow?

Above all, keep on pickin'…

PRACTICE ROLLS + LICKS FOR JOHN HARDY

FORWARD/REVERSE

HAMMER

I M I M T I M T · I M T I M T I · T I M T I M T

John Hardy – G

Intro

THE Bob Altschuler WORKSHOP

INTRODUCTION

At Banjo Camp North, I had a roommate Ken who elected to take beginning bluegrass workshops throughout the weekend. Like most camps, at BCN you self-select your level and your program. As this was my fourth camp and I had been studying bluegrass for a year, I followed the intermediate program. It also gave me a chance to hear a lot of Tony Trischka, Alan Munde, and Bill Evans.

After dinner, there was a faculty concert followed by breakout jams in various buildings. Ken would come into the dorm, excited about his instructor Bob Altschuler, and take out his banjo to run through some of the chord changes he had learned. I had an open slot one morning and sat in on Bob's class. Often I've regretted that it was the only class of Bob's I was able to take. In one session, in simple, clear terms, Bob presented ideas I hadn't picked up on before.

I walked into his class knowing the three major chord positions and their minor variations and could play pretty confidently on the lower fretboard. I couldn't transpose keys without my capo and was a little dicey once I passed the tenth fret. I walked out, an hour and a half later, and I was able to back up pretty much any song on my banjo, in any key, all along the fretboard, from the nut to the rim. I can still do it today, thanks to Bob's simple rules and his presentation. (Check out Rule Five in his workshop and see if it doesn't get rid of any lingering jam anxiety you might feel.)

In the following workshop, you'll pick up on how clearly Altschuler spells out his rules and how the tabs reinforce the ideas. What you won't get is how patient and kind he is. A big guy, towering over the students for the most part, Bob ran the toughest segment of the Banjo Camp North program. Even though he had the largest classes—and some challenging locations on campus—he worked with each of his students, answered all questions, and hung in past midnight at the beginner bluegrass jams. I attended only one of those jams. What I saw were a couple of dozen new bluegrass banjo players, late at night, happily backing up songs thrown at them randomly by Bob and his associate Rich Stillman, hitting all the chord changes, whether vamping or rolling.

Bob Altschuler, a banjo player for more than 30 years, records primarily with the Dyer Switch band (www.dyerswitch. com), and performs at bluegrass festivals and in concert in the northeast, midwest, and south. His banjo style merges traditional bluegrass with blues and jazz influences. You can see some of his instructional articles online at *Mel Bay Banjo Sessions* magazine (www.banjosessions. com). Featured on National Public Radio and on radio and TV commercials, Altschuler is a deeply committed teacher. He lives in the upstate New York mountain area.

LESSON: FINDING CHORDS—A FRETBOARD ROAD MAP

The key to finding chords and chord progressions anywhere on the neck is learning just a few simple rules. Seeing the neck as a whole (not as unrelated pieces) and understanding repeating patterns, moveable chords, and progressions will help boost you up to the next level of playing. This fingerboard road map will help you create breaks and improvise. It's especially suited for backup and playing with other musicians, which means you play backup most of the time. Fingerboard knowledge is as important as learning breaks to songs, and will expand your ability to jam with other musicians.

There are logical, easy-to-learn rules and landmarks for finding chords and progressions. These are useful for finding the primary I-IV-V chords (like G-C-D in the key of G, or C-F-G in the key of C) in different places on the neck. Many songs consist of only these I-IV-V chords (see the I, IV, and V chords in the G and C scales, above right). I've had beginning students who were able to find chords and play solid basic backup in jams after learning just some of the rules.

First, here's some background about chords:

- Since there are 12 notes (A through G, plus sharps and flats), they repeat on the same string every 12 frets (one octave). It's like playing keys in order on a piano.
- Like notes, major chords go in alphabetical order, from A to G and then start to repeat. There are sharps (#) and flats (b) between all chords (and notes) except for B to C and E to F.
- A major scale has 8 notes (do, re, mi, fa, so, la, ti, do).
- Major chords are made from the 1, 3, and 5 notes of a scale (for example, G major is G, B, and D notes; C major is C, E, and G notes).
- You can also find the I, IV, and V (and other) chords in any key by using the scale.

- Here are two examples of scales:

	1	2	3	4	5	6	7	8
Key of G	G	A	B	C	D	E	F#	G

	1	2	3	4	5	6	7	8
Key of C	C	D	E	F	G	A	B	C

- There are three chord shapes, or positions, to form a major chord in G tuning. By moving these chord shapes along the neck, you can play all major chords and progressions in all keys.
- All three positions for any major chord consist of the same 1, 3, and 5 notes of the scale in different order, sometimes 3-5-1 or 5-1-3, for example. Some notes are played more than once in a chord, since there are three notes and you are playing four strings.
- By changing certain finger positions and notes in any major chord, you can play minors, sevenths, and other chords. These chord positions are also moveable and follow fretboard progressions, like the major chords.
- The F position looks like a triangle pointed upward, the D position is a downward pointing triangle, and the barre is a straight line across the fingerboard. Start with G, C, and D chords, and learn these chord shapes all over the neck until you can play them automatically. (In the chord diagrams, I=left index finger, M=middle finger, R=ring, and P=pinky).

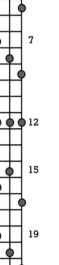

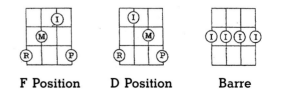

F Position   **D Position**   **Barre**

Let's play a barre chord and move it up the neck one fret at a time. If you think of the open G chord as a barre chord and move up one fret, you get G#. Move up another fret and you have an A chord, then A#, B, C, C#, D, D#, E, F, F#, and then another G chord at fret 12 (one octave up). The chords keep repeating after fret 12.

If we start with an F-position F chord at frets 1–3 and move up one fret, we have F#, then G, G#, etc.

There is another F chord 12 frets above the start (one octave) at frets 13–15, and then F#, G, etc. repeat until the fingerboard runs out.

If we start with a D position D chord at frets 2–4, we can again move up the neck in chord order (D#, E, F, F#, etc.), until we get to another D-position D chord 12 frets up at frets 14–16. The chords then continue to repeat. OK, enough theory?

Moving Up the Fretboard

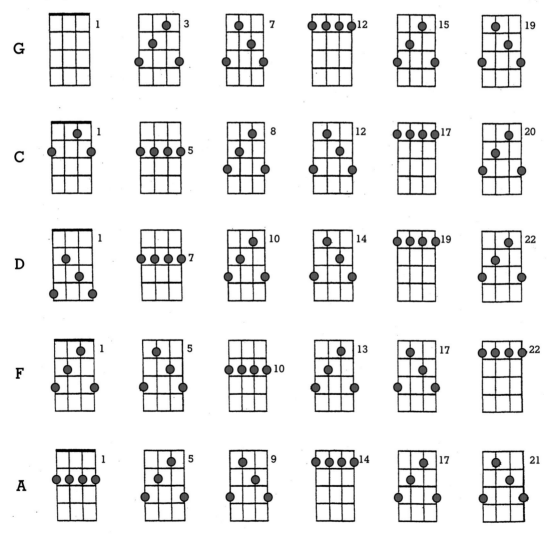

THE BOB ALTSCHULER WORKSHOP

❖ THE SIX RULES

Here are six practical rules for finding chords and progressions. The first three rules will help you *find the same chord in different places,* and the next three rules will help you *locate the I, IV, and V chords in any key.*

Rule One: To find the same chord in the same chord shape up the neck, move the position up 12 frets.

For example, there are F-position G chords at frets 3–5 and frets 15–17. There are D-position D chords at frets 2–4 and frets 14–16.

Rule Two: Another way (among several) to find the same chord, but this time in two different positions, is to play the D-position chord and then move up three frets from the top end of the chord and make a barre position.

For example, play a D-position G at frets 7–9, and then a barred G at fret 12. Or, make a D-position C chord at frets 1–2 (your 3rd string finger for the D position is knocked off the neck) and then barre a C at fret 5. I use this often in my playing.

Rule Three: To find the next higher position of a chord from an F position, move it up four frets and change it to a D position. This is very useful for backup! (Hint: Slide up and use strings 1 and 4 as a "track" while you switch your fingers on strings 2 and 3. Also, if you move up three frets and make a barre chord, you get the same chord again.)

For example, play an F-position G chord at frets 3–5, and then a D-position G chord at frets 7–9 and keep moving up the fingerboard for a barre-position G chord at the 12th fret.

Now let's look at some easy ways for you to find the "right" chord in a box, or small space, on the fretboard, which is what you'd be doing most of the time.

Rule Four: A way to play the I, IV, and V chords in a short space (four frets) is to start with the F-position chord and barre at the upper fret of the chord by flattening your ring finger (your middle finger may also flatten) to get the IV chord. Then, move down (toward the peg head) one fret to a D position to play the V chord. (Hint: Slide down and use strings 1 and 4 as a "track" while you switch fingers on strings 2 and 3).

For example, play an F-position G chord at frets 3–5, barre at fret 5 to get a C (the IV chord), and then move down one fret to a D position at frets 2–4 to play D (the V chord). Or play an F-position C chord at frets 8–10, barre at fret 10 to get an F (the IV chord), and then move down one fret to a D position at frets 7–9 to play G (the V chord).

Rule Five: Another way to play the I-IV-V chords in a short space (six frets) is to start with the D-position chord, and move up one fret to an F position to play the IV chord. To play the V chord, move that F position up two frets. For example, play a D-position G chord at frets 7–9, move up one fret and change to an F-position C chord (the IV chord), and then move this position up two more frets to a D, the V chord. (As in Rules Three and Four, slide between positions, using strings 1 and 4 as a "track" while you switch fingers on strings 2 and 3.)

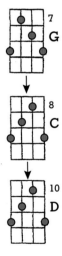

Using Rules Four and Five, you can play the I-IV-V chords without even knowing what the IV and V chords are (although you should), as long as you know the I chord.

Rule Six: A third way to play the I-IV-V chords in a short space (five frets) is to start with a barre chord and then play a D position, starting on the barred fret to get the IV chord. Move that D position up two frets to play the V chord.

For example, play a barred G chord at fret 12, and then play a D position at frets 12–14 to get a C chord. Next, move the C chord up two frets to get a D chord at frets 14–16.

There are other ways to find chords and progressions on the neck. The six rules in this workshop are a good starting point.

I recommend learning Rule Three first, which is great for vamping in backup. Then learn Rule Four, which is a good place to start for the I-IV-V chords. Practice these one at a time (a jam is a good place to try things out) until your left hand motion is easy and fluid. Then, go on to the next rule and incorporate it into your playing.

To play a basic break at a jam, pick right-hand roll patterns while you change to the correct chords. Or, you can play vamping or other backup patterns while using the rules to locate the chords in a song. Also, learn the I-IV-V chords in different keys (especially in G, C, and D) and then use the rules to find them. If you know the I chord, you can find the other chords. (Hint: To figure out the chords that are being played, watch the guitar player! Learn what G, C, D, and other guitar chord shapes look like.)

The more you play these positions and progressions, the easier it will be to build on what you know. This gives you many possibilities for backup, breaks, improvisation, and the most important activity for a banjo picker—playing with other musicians.

Happy picking!

Forming minor and seventh chords from the 3 basic major chord positions

POSITION

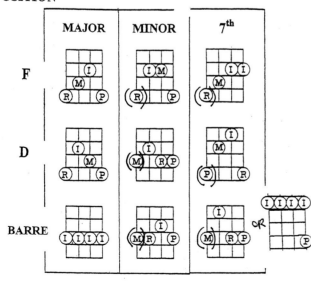

THE Rich Stillman WORKSHOP

INTRODUCTION

For a while, Rich Stillman flirted with the dark side. A born musician, for years he would ply his electronic trade, experimenting with, evaluating, and implementing systems and services for clients and employees like the Harvard Business School.

It's hard to say when his recovery began, but Rich found a banjo at a garage sale 30 years ago. And while he continued to produce magical electronic effects for his clients—and experiment with such arcana as electronic sound enhancement (removing surface noise from 78s and cylinders) and stereo photography—banjo claimed his soul and brought him into the light.

When I met Rich, I knew nothing of his past. All I saw was a blazing fast banjo picker, a friendly, helpful guy who would show up at the jams and help move things along. I did hear him play with Eric Weissberg and Janet Davis at a workshop, but my schedule was

jammed and I didn't catch any of his classes. At the end, from watching him work in the jams, he was the guy I wanted to show me right-hand roll technique, and we talked about ways of hooking up. Bringing his workshop into Blue Mountain Banjo Camp is the beginning, and an opportunity for you to learn some bluegrass picking from a master teacher who has been under the radar.

One of New England's premier bluegrass banjo pickers, Rich walked away with the New England five-string banjo championship two years running and is six-time bluegrass banjo contest winner at the Lowell Banjo and Fiddle Festivals. Today, he is a full-time musician—performing with Southern Rail—writes songs and bluegrass commentaries, and teaches privately and at banjo camps.

His dark side hasn't completely disappeared, however. One option he offers his students is distance learning via web cam over the Internet. For information, you can check out his website, www.waystation.com. For an advance taste of the Rich Stillman magic, here's his workshop designed to bring your bluegrass picking up a notch. Shazam!

LESSON: BLUEGRASS TECHNIQUE TUNE-UP

Most people, no matter how long they've been playing banjo, have developed bad habits (or failed to develop good ones) that limit their playing. Sometimes it's a lick that just won't flow, or frustration when trying to play fast, or one hard-to-play passage that keeps an entire tune out of the repertoire. Many people attribute these limits to a "plateau" and keep practicing with their old habits, waiting—sometimes for years—for problems to magically clear up. The following techniques should help supply some of that magic.

Part One: The Right Hand

Great banjo players just sound special. Their notes are impeccably timed and have a momentum that carries the listener along, as if there's a thread that ties them all together. The unique sound of three-finger banjo comes partly from playing almost every note on a different string than the one before, so each one gets a chance to fade away while the next note or two is being played. A pro player's smoothness comes from right-hand motion that's as continuous as possible, so each note has the longest possible time to fade.

✹ THE BICYCLE

Diagnosis

Get out your banjo, and play a forward roll—not the eight-note roll that you learned when you first started playing, but a continuous TIMTIMTIMTIM on the 5th, 2nd, and 1st strings. Get it as smooth as you can, and start watching your right hand. You should see all three fingers moving in circles, without stopping. Your index and middle fingers should look like two legs pedaling a bicycle. When you pedal, your feet are forced to go around in continuous circles; you want your fingerpicks to behave exactly the same way. If one finger stays stationary above the strings, then reaches down to play a note and returns to that "parked" position to wait for

its next assignment, your playing won't sound smooth, especially when you start speeding up. When you play fast, your fingers may also tense up prematurely and limit your playing speed. That stationary time between notes means your fingers have to move faster during the stroke, so your overall speed will suffer from that alone.

The fix

Keep playing that forward roll, and slow it down to the point where you can visually follow what your right hand is doing. Don't let your fingers stop during the playing cycle. If you can't get continuous circles out of a forward roll, play each finger individually (MMMMMM, IIIIIIII, TTTTTTTT) until you get used to the motion, and then put the roll back together. After you've got the continuous motion working on a forward roll, start playing your most familiar songs using this technique and see what happens.

What should happen

This exercise should yield several benefits. First, you should immediately hear your playing get smoother and more flowing. Second, you should be able to play faster, since your fingers are actually moving slower now that they're not wasting time standing still between notes. Third, you should find it much easier to play familiar tunes at different speeds. This is a surprising side benefit that happens because it's easier to change the speed of a continuous circular motion than a complex motion that starts and stops.

Got it? Practice that for a while, and then move on to the next exercise.

Emphasizing the melody

The flurry of notes produced by a bluegrass banjo is, by nature, confusing to listen to. Unlike most other instruments, the important notes of the melody are mixed in with many other notes that create harmony and fill the time between the melody notes. It's one of the factors that makes three-finger banjo such an interesting style, but it also puts a great deal of responsibility on the player.

If you're trying to play a familiar tune, your audience will probably be able to pick the melody out of the soup. If it's a tune they haven't heard before, or if you're improvising a new melody for an old tune, they may get lost trying to distinguish between the important notes and the filler. Without a melody to follow, your audience will walk away saying, "all that banjo music sounds the same." And you might, too.

If you don't want this to happen to you, make your melody notes stand out by playing them louder than the rest. Doing this requires an extra measure of control over your right hand. As a first exercise, try playing this two-measure roll:

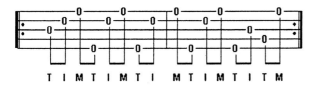

T I M T I M T I   M T I M T I T M

Play it over and over again until it's smooth and automatic, and every note sounds the same. If it sounds choppy, go back and review the last section on bicycle motion.

While you're playing this lick, pay special attention to the syncopation of the notes. Syncopation is a slight variation between the timing of notes that emphasizes every other note. If you play this roll with syncopation, it will sound like this:

DAH dah DAH dah DAH dah DAH dah DAH dah DAH dah DAH dah DAH dah

That's NOT what you want, since it forces the emphasis onto every other note, and those may not be the melody notes. The timing you give to every note should sound the same, so that lick will sound like this:

dah dah dah dah dah dah dah dah dah dah dah dah dah dah dah dah

Got it? Now it's time to add the magic ingredient. Choose one of your three fingers, and play the roll again, making that finger play its notes louder than the other two. You can use any finger for this—you'll end up doing this exercise with each one.

You'll notice two things when you try this. First, the notes your preferred finger is playing will become the dominant notes of the roll, and the other ones will start sounding like filler. Second, you'll hear a rhythm that emphasizes every third note through most of the roll. For example, if you start with your middle finger, your roll will sound like this:

dah dah DAH dah dah DAH dah dah DAH dah dah DAH dah dah dah DAH

Emphasizing the thumb will give you this:

DAH dah dah DAH dah dah DAH dah dah DAH dah dah DAH dah DAH dah

The magic happens when you carry this rhythm beyond the first measure. You're creating a three-note emphasis that's at odds with the up/down, 2/4 rhythm of most bluegrass. It's the tension created by this shifting rhythm that's at the core of the special sound of three-finger banjo. Carrying that rhythm through two or more measures is what makes many banjo breaks memorable. Note that the syncopation we talked about earlier is in direct conflict with this rhythm—it forces every other note to be emphasized, so the banjo is producing two different rhythms that make no sense when heard together. This is why it's so important to be able to play evenly, without syncopation.

Play around with this for a while, until the three-note emphasis is pretty natural. Got it? Now it's time to put this rhythmic stuff to practical use.

If you're already playing tunes, pick out one that you play well. Choose one that has forward rolls in it, which lets out tunes like "Cripple Creek" that are made purely of alternating thumb rolls. The alternating thumb roll is ready-made for two-note rhythm. It sounds great with syncopation, which emphasizes the same rhythm as the roll. Pick a tune like "Little Darling Pal of Mine" that has lots of forward roll. If you have tablature for your tune, make a copy of it, and get a highlighting pen. Go through the tab and pick out the melody notes. For at least part of the tune, you'll find the melody on every third note of a roll. Use your highlighter to mark these melody notes, so your tab looks like this:

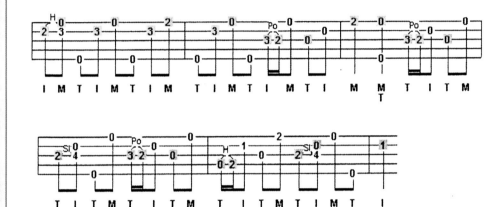

This tab is the first phrase of "Sunny Side of the Mountain." Notice that, unlike the forward roll exercise, the melody notes in this real-world tab move from finger to finger. In some parts of the tab, two fingers carry the melody at the same time, adding even more interest to the rhythm. Play this tab, or the tune of your choice, with emphasis on the melody notes, and an interesting thing will happen for your audience (and probably for you). The filler notes will start to sound like background, just an indistinguishable (but good-sounding) hum. That will leave the melody out front and easy to hear. Do this right, and you'll be able to play any melody you want, familiar or not, and take your audience along for the ride. Even better, the rhythms you create by emphasizing your melody on every third note will make your sound more interesting and exciting.

Part Two: The Left Hand

Here's something else that sets great players apart: No matter how hard the lick, they look like they're not even working. This impression comes mostly from their left hand movements, which always look relaxed and accurate—because they are. Here are some techniques that will help you get that smooth left hand.

✺ ONE FINGER AT A TIME

The most important technique for a smooth left hand is also the simplest: Don't try to put an entire chord shape or position down at once. Focus on one finger at a time, and everything will end up in the right place, quickly and accurately. Start with the first finger you're going to play, and put the rest down in the order you'll play them. Not only will you be able to place one finger more accurately than several at once, but each finger will act as a platform that makes aiming the subsequent fingers easier. You'll also be more relaxed because you won't have to rush to place all your fingers on the strings before playing the first one.

Think of the left-hand position as a wave, with each left hand finger getting placed just before the corresponding right-hand finger plays that string. Start out slow, since you'll have to think about how you'll build the position as you do it. After some practice, this technique will become second nature.

✺ GUIDE FINGERS

Try this experiment. Put a G chord down at the 5th fret. Now, without looking at the fingerboard, lift all your fingers off the strings and form a D chord at the 4th fret. Play that chord. Did that work? Now play that same G chord, and lift all your fingers, except the one on the 1st string. Slide that finger back to the 4th fret and form the D chord. Easier? I thought so.

Lifting all your fingers off the strings removes any connection you have to the fingerboard, and leaves your hand floating in space. Leave one finger touching a string, and that string becomes a rail that guides the rest of your fingers where they belong. Instead of trying to move your hands in three dimensions, using a guide finger means you only have to move in one dimension. Aim that finger for the fret it will occupy in the new chord, and you can build the whole position around it.

The good news is that almost every position change offers at least one finger that covers the same string in the new and old positions. Use that finger as your guide, and even the hardest position changes—the ones that involve movements of five or more frets—become far easier. This is particularly true if you follow the next piece of advice.

✺ LOOK BEFORE YOU LEAP

If you're moving a long way on the neck, do you need to watch your left hand? Not exactly. If you follow your left hand with your eyes, the frets become a blur, and you can't tell where to stop. Instead of watching your hand, look at the fret your left hand (and its guide finger) are aiming at. When your hand comes racing up or down the fingerboard, you'll be looking at its stopping point.

❖ COVER YOUR MOVES

One final piece of left-hand advice: Plan your moves, especially the big ones, carefully. As I mentioned in the right-hand part of this workshop, the overlapping sound of successive banjo notes is one reason three-finger playing sounds unique. To keep that overlap, you need to hold a left-hand position long enough to let that position's last note fade away into the background as new notes replace it. But don't hold the note too long, or you won't have time to move to the new position without a very fast and difficult left-hand move. Finding the right time to make a move takes practice, but two things can make it easier.

The first is the prevalence of open strings in most banjo breaks. An open string is like a free pass to move your left hand, play the open note, and start your left-hand move pretty much anytime you want after that.

The second thing: If there's no open string, make the best of the situation by turning your guide finger move into a slide. It's amazing how many really good-sounding slides are actually done out of necessity, so there isn't an interruption in the flow of notes.

❖ THANKS FOR LISTENING

If you've read this far, thank you. I hope you found something that improves your playing. These techniques have helped virtually every one of my students, and I hope they've helped you, too.

THE Alan Munde WORKSHOP

INTRODUCTION

This is not the only time you'll see Alan Munde. He's the tall, smiling prankster in the baseball cap and yellow rain jacket at the Music Hall Opera House production (page 116). You also might know him from his many records, banjo instruction books, and performances, or from his own bluegrass camp in Levelland, Texas.

By any measure, as a performer or a teacher, Alan Munde is one of the five-string banjo giants. Born in Oklahoma, Munde first came to national prominence as banjo player with Jimmy Martin's band in the late '60s. After a few years, he joined the band Country Gazette and started publishing his tabs, instruction books, and a series of solo and collaborative CDs, with musicians like Sam Bush. He taught bluegrass and country music at famed South Plains College in Levelland, Texas, for two decades, and retired in 2007 to start touring with his new band, Alan Munde Gazette. Part of the Levelland program is the big, popular Camp Bluegrass program held annually on the college campus.

From such a towering figure, the advice to trust yourself is most welcome. "One of the things people get into," says Munde, "is believing there's only one way to do this. One way to put on picks, one way to hold your hand. They got it from people they admire. There are two things going on. As a student of bluegrass, every time you play something it's like taking a pilgrimage. On the one side are the people you admire. On the other side, you're an individual, this is your art, and you're responsible to move on and do it your way.

"Don't get caught in the idea that you're only a student copying the master and you have to only do it the way he did it and create music only in his mold. You're an individual, and you can try to be him, but you will never make it. It can cause a lot of conflict."

Considering the demand for his time, I asked him why he taught at banjo camps and participated in projects like this one. "I didn't invent any of this. The value of banjo camp is a way to pass along this music, share the history of yourself, and rethink what you're really doing. It's a chance to convey what one needs to do in order to play this instrument."

In this workshop, Alan takes us through one of the most critical of all skills for a bluegrass player— picking the melody out of rolls. Think of Earl Scruggs' admonition "to play the syllables" as you follow this modern master's guidance.

LESSON: ROLL LOGIC

Banjo playing—stringed instruments in general— can be confusing because you can get the same note in several places on your instrument, and each one of the choices you make affects what roll possibilities you can use. Where you place a note on the instrument is important.

Some people think that all of music-making is just intuitive—you just bang around on this thing and sounds start to emerge. You talk to other musicians, and they play the way they feel. How do they get to this point where it just comes out?

✳ THINK ABOUT IT

Most musicians I know of didn't get to where they are without thinking about what they're doing. So at some point you have to sit down and think about what's going on musically. After you figure that out, you can forget it and go on to the mechanics. You have to think, "I want to play a G note on a roll—what string should I put it on?" There could be a lot of reasons to make that decision, and you have to be aware of those reasons so, to a certain extent, you can control what you're doing.

When musicians say "I just play the way I feel," they mean, "Of all the things I've done before and practiced and can do, that's what I chose to do." It's kind of like learning a language. Selecting a note is like selecting a word. When you talk, you say things you "feel like saying," but they don't come out of nowhere; your words and ideas come from the past, from grammar, from all the things you do to get socialized in a language, and it's the same way with music. You know, I feel like playing the melody here, but I could play it there. Because I rehearsed and practiced it there in the past, I select that position to play the melody. In part, that's how, in my estimation, "playing how I feel" happens. It's very clever people putting in a lot of time doing it.

Let's check out two forms of the G scale. Which one is right? They're both right. I've noticed that a lot of times banjo pickers play up and down a string instead of across. Try for yourself.

Now let's talk about some practical examples using melodies emerging from rolls. Students of the bluegrass style of banjo spend many hours learning, rehearsing, and performing the several roll patterns that make up

Notes of the G scale on the B (2nd) string

B	C	D	E		F#	G	A	B	C	D	E	F#	G	A
0	1	3	5		7	8	10	12	13	15	17	19	20	21

Notes of the G scale on the G (3rd) string

G	A	B	C	D	E		F#	G	A	B	C	D	E
0	2	4	5			7	9	11	12	14	16	17	19	21

the core of the style. But what is really happening with those rolls? How do melodies survive in all those notes? What part of the roll is the melody and what part is not? What are the notes that are not the melody?

Bluegrass banjo playing has a certain mechanical element about it. The right-hand roll is like a machine that repeats its function unfailingly, while the left hand feeds information into the process at precise, timed places. Melodies are embedded in the roll in specific locations.

Looking at the tab of a forward roll, you'll see the first, fourth, and seventh notes of the roll most generally are where the melody is placed. The other notes are rhythmic and harmonic filler around the melody.

This roll can play up to three melody notes per measure. Fortunately, many melodies or parts of melodies are organized in that fashion. (This is a generalized view. As a player becomes more comfortable with the style, there are many ways to use the rolls to present more nuanced musical ideas.)

Now here's a forward roll on a G string. Try using the notes of the G scale located on the second and third strings, and embed these scale notes into the forward roll to create melodies of your own…or try the examples.

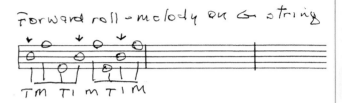

Play through the melodies of "Long, Long Ago" and "Wildwood Flower." Compare the melody of the top line with the melody placed into the forward roll. Note that the fourth note of the roll falls on the "and" of the second beat of the measure. When a melody note is moved from a strong beat to the weak beat, it's referred to as *syncopation*. This happens in bluegrass banjo playing as a function of some of the rolls—the forward roll in this instance.

Each roll has its different pres-entation of a melody, and by being aware of that aspect of style, you can create your own unique arrangement of the music.

Thank you. Think for yourself and have fun with it.

Wildwood Flower

THE Old-Time HORSE & BUGGY
SLIDE TOUR

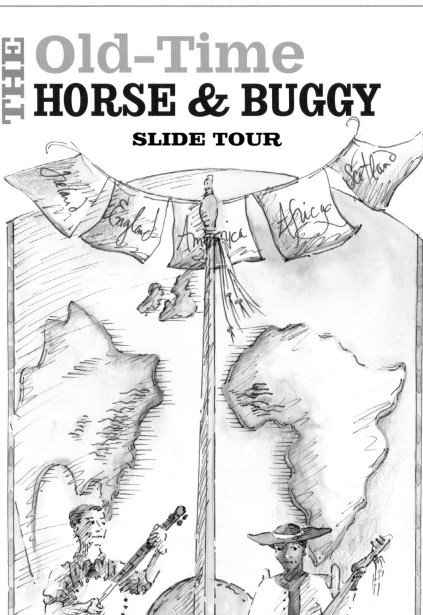

Those of you who took the Bluegrass Express tour are in for a change of pace. Instead of a speedy express roaring down the tracks, we're going to climb aboard a horse and buggy and take some back trails, riding real slow over the bumps, to visit the back-home world of old-time music.

Even though some of the freshest sounds you'll hear come out of this music, it's called *old-time* (or *roots*) music, mostly to differentiate it from its kissin' cuz'n, the much younger and brasher bluegrass music with which it shares some antecedents and forms. So before we get to our first destination, I'm going to take a detour to describe the terrain we're crossing.

Bluegrass vs. Old-Time

The divide between the two main streams of contemporary banjo music, old-time and bluegrass, is wide. You don't want to be wearing fingerpicks on this tour. Both types of music share country and folk roots. So when bluegrass split off into electrifying pop performance directions, it appalled die-hard old-time musicians.

In general, bluegrass is faster, louder, flashier. Bluegrass tunes are largely created by contemporary songwriters. Bluegrass musicians take individual performance breaks, singers use close vocal harmonies, and in the beginning, everyone would crowd around an onstage mike in performances for festival crowds instead of sitting back on the porch and playing together with one another. And while old-time is mostly fiddle-based, bluegrass is characterized by driving rhythms and rolls—the improvised licks and leads of the banjo, mandolin, and guitar.

The trauma suffered by old-time musicians in the face of this change was something like what the folk purists in the early sixties felt when Dylan went electric at Newport. When bluegrass emerged from old-time banjo, lots of old-time country musicians felt betrayed. Some traditionalists still do.

Old-Time Roots

Although there aren't universally accepted definitions of old-time music, there are guidelines. This music comes out of the handmade folk traditions—from the Appalachians and Ozarks, as well as the Red River Valley and the Rift Valley. And that means no amplification, and the kind of instruments folks would play when they're off the grid in Senegal or in isolated mountain cabins or cattle roundups—fiddle, banjo, guitar, jugs, bones, stand-up bass, jaw's harp, and washboards.

As a drum with strings, the banjo plays a special role here by providing both backup rhythm and melody. Much of old-time music derives from fiddle tunes, which makes banjo rhythm backup essential. In the country, a "band" put together for a frolic often consisted only of fiddle and banjo.

Many musicians who play mountain music, "hillbilly" music, roots music by any name, don't call it "old-time." Even its characteristic clawhammer style—employing a semirigid, down-picking wrist and forearm motion—goes by a number of different names, *frailing* being the most popular. The way old-time banjo is played often takes its name from the musician's own locality.

◀ Jan Davidson

Jan Davidson, director of the John C. Campbell Folk School located near his hometown of Murphy, North Carolina, when asked what he called his frailing style, said, "I don't know. Here we just call it the Murphy lick."

Old-time is traditional folk music, and consists of songs passed along through oral tradition for the most part, with the same African and western European roots that formed bluegrass. But there the similarity ends and an often bitter division begins.

And if you think bluegrass harks back to Civil War days and rose up along with bib overalls and early railroads, you'd be off the mark by a full century. Instead of Lincoln and Robert E. Lee, think Roosevelt and Churchill. Union and Confederate boys did take their banjos along to war, but what they played was old-time music, often variations of African-American plantation songs, minstrel tunes, and Scotch-Irish folk ballads. As late as 1956, Earl Scruggs' wife Louise reportedly had no idea what a New York DJ was talking about when he called to request some "bluegrass" music.

Blue Ridge Old-Time Music Week

OK, we're hitched up and ready to roll. First stop on this bumpy horse-and-buggy slide show tour of old-time banjo is Mars Hill, North Carolina, the birthplace of banjo-picking musicologist Bascom Lamar Lundsford, where, in his honor, Mars Hill College annually hosts the Blue Ridge Old-Time Music Week. A major event, drawing high-level old-time musicians to teach and perform, BROTMW is fairly typical of other banjo camps with one important exception—it is a lot quieter.

Small groups of students were jamming around the Mars Hill College campus, but gone was the raucous lead break of a resonator-backed banjo, the "electric guitar" of a bluegrass band. In its place you could hear the harmonious blending of a country string ensemble. It was calm. People played together, in unison, without individual solo breaks.

◄ Laura Boosinger

A beginning old-time banjo class, taught by Laura Boosinger, moved almost sedately through its first steps. Boosinger, an international performer with multiple CD releases, demonstrated basic clawhammer technique and simple chord forms to a mixed group of retired people and teenagers.

Students barely looked at the tab she had handed out—most just followed Boosinger as she played the rhythmic, simple melody line. This was the second session and most students already had the hang of it. That was one apparent difference in the old-time style. The down-picking, syncopated strum comes naturally to the human arm and hand. Many new bluegrass pickers, at this stage, would still be fumbling with the forward roll and trying to untangle fingers.

Typical of old-time musicians, Boosinger plays multiple instruments. Equally at home with guitar, mountain dulcimer, and Autoharp, she has recorded with David Holt and George Shuffler, among many others, and on her own. Best known for a clear voice that just seems to be at home with the simple old-time melodies, Laura is also a terrific dancer, and she shows off her clogging most Saturday nights in the summer at Asheville's Shindig on the Green.

Bob Carlin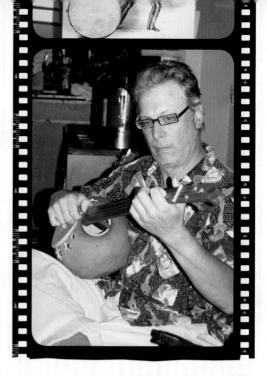

Bob Carlin, a world-renowned old-time banjo headliner, scholar, and teacher, teaching at this BROTW session. Between classes, down at the Mars Hill cafeteria, he's talking about the growing attraction of old-time music.

"I think that open-back old-time clawhammer is more popular right now than it has ever been since after WW II, since the sixties. It's bigger now than during the folk revival. The reason? A combination of factors. One is the "O Brother, Where Art Thou" effect. And there are improved instruments, more companies making these good-quality, affordable open-backs. There are also more teaching materials available right now, so all of this contributes.

"More importantly, I think the current 20-something generation has some commonality with my generation when I was 20. There's the same increased awareness and the desire to play things that have roots and connection to people—to music that is emotionally expressive. Go to one of the big fiddlers' conventions. Of 4,000 people, 2,000 are under 30, and that's a huge change."

Do You Know the Chocolate Drops?

I was beginning to get the picture, but it took a chance conversation with Hilary Dirlam, director of Blue Ridge Old-Time Music Week, before I would take off my fingerpicks and get serious about old-time. After cruising the campus, interviewing teachers and students, I asked her where all the African-American banjo players were. I had seen none at the camps or schools or festivals, not in the South and not in the North. She said, "Do you know the Carolina Chocolate Drops?"

I didn't, and if you have not yet heard this old-time band in action, right after you leave camp, you might want to pick up one of their CDs or head for your computer and dial up YouTube to catch one of their performances. You'll see and hear a young, very powerful string band in action and get a small taste of the past and future of old-time. It's hard to say why that video clip of a young band playing an old-timey song in string-band style of the 1920s was the tipping point, but their version of "Georgia Buck Is Dead" opened up the ancient and limitless world of roots music to me.

The Minstrel Connection

Starting in the 1820s and extending well into the beginning of the 20th century, song-and-dance minstrel music dominated American pop culture. Until this luncheon conversation with Hilary, I was as oblivious to minstrelsy as I was to Celtic music.

Whoa! Looks like our horse has thrown a shoe. We have to pull this buggy over to the side for a bit. While we're getting her re-shod, let's sit alongside this road a minute and talk about the minstrel times, and I'll tell you a true story.

You're too young to know the song that went:

Wheel about an' turn about, and 'do jus so
Eb'ry time I wheel about, I jump Jim Crow

The chorus that launched America's first internationally popular song led in a straight line through ragtime and blues, to bluegrass and rock-and-roll, but left behind the source.

In 1828, Thomas Dartmouth "Daddy" Rice, so the story goes, saw a crippled black man dancing and singing the song that would come to be known as "Jump Jim Crow" to an audience that laughed at his antics. Rice, a performer who already appeared on stage in blackface, was so impressed he bought the man's clothes, and incorporated his song and dance into his own act.

The tune became so popular in the United States and worldwide that, in 1841, when U.S. ambassador John Lloyd Stephens arrived in Merida, Yucatan, he was greeted by the local brass band playing "Jump Jim Crow" under the mistaken impression that it was America's national anthem.

African-American banjo player, c 1875

White musicians in "black face." Courtesy of Jim Bollman

The Minstrel Movement

Even though the minstrel craze wouldn't move into high gear until 1843, when the Virginia Minstrels introduced their rapid-fire songs, skits, dances, and variety acts performed by white actors in blackface, this story of Jump Jim Crow—the appropriation and exploitation of African-American slave culture—would be repeated, in one form or another, well into the twentieth century.

Music critic Robert Christgau makes the case that early minstrel music has a lot in common with rock-and-roll. "Like minstrelsy, rock-and-roll posed not just a racial danger, but a class danger...it delivered pop music from status anxieties and polite facades. It made a role model of the unkempt rebel. And, by finding simple tunes in the three-chord storehouse of folk modality, it cleared a space for unencumbered beat. Got it? Now ask yourself how much of the rock-and-roll description can be applied to minstrelsy and vice versa."

There may be no practical reason to know the "Jump Jim Crow" story, but 200 years of minstrelsy is an inextricable part of the context of American folk music and the history of the banjo, America's instrument. The rhythmic roots and clawhammer style of old-time music are clearly African.

It's possible that the degradation of African-American slave culture on stage, portrayed by white minstrels in blackface, dressed in shabby, comic clothes and bashed-in hats, is partly responsible for the wholesale absence of African-American banjo players from festival stages and banjo camps. Maybe not. It's possible that young African-Americans—like the rest of young Americans—have better things to do or are simply distracted by the glut of electronic globalized schlock in the culture.

A New Generation

Dom Flemons, the brilliant busker, stringed instrument scholar, and multi-instrument performer with the Chocolate Drops, thinks it has more to do with generations:

"African-American kids and old folks have no problem with our music. It's the ones in between who aren't that far out of the country and are just making it in urban culture who say, 'What do you want to play that kind of music for?'"

Middle: Dom Flemons and Rhiannon Giddens
Bottom: Justin Robinson

Young urban crowds have enthusiastically welcomed the Carolina Chocolate Drops from the Brooklyn waterfront to the San Francisco Bay Area. This is an important development because, when you talk about root music—the root that makes the heart swell, blood boil, and feet dance—that music is African to the core. Without awareness of the source, it's separated from its root. The Carolina Chocolate Drops musicians, with their youthful exuberance and enormous ability, are bringing one stream of that music back home.

Looks like we're all re-shod. Detour over. Let's get our horse back in harness and buggy on over to the Swannanoa Gathering.

Old-Time Music Week at the Swannanoa Gathering

When you talk old-time music, age matters. And while there have been old-time folk music schools since at least the Old Town School of Folk Music in Chicago in 1957, the Swannanoa Gathering on the Warren Wilson College campus in Asheville, North Carolina, may be the oldest university-based, old-time music program that includes training in instruments. Growing out of a program started by David Holt in 1978, the Gathering is a series of week-long summer workshops that focus on various areas.

Have a look around the campus as we find a hitching post to tie up for a few hours.

Warren Wilson College

Warren Wilson College is located in the Swannanoa Valley on the outskirts of Asheville, in the foothills of the Blue Ridge Mountains. Far as you can see, these old buildings, pavilions, barns, and trails are part of a 1,000-acre vision that started in the 1890s. Warren Wilson is a four-year college, but you'll never see its team at the Cotton Bowl…or for that matter at any bowl. There's no football here. The required triad at Warren Wilson stands for academics, work, and service. The 800 or so students on campus spend 15 hours a week on assigned campus work, some of it taking place on the college's 300-acre farm, some in the computer lab; others participate in community-service programs along with a full class load.

During the summer the campus is largely turned over to several weeks of the Swannanoa Gathering, bringing together musicians with various interests. This is Old-Time Music Week, and you can hear the banjos and fiddles playing under the trees and in the classrooms.

Phil Jamison ▶

Our guide to the Swannanoa Gathering is banjo-picking, clog-dancing, old-time scholar and director of the Old-Time Music Week at the Gathering, Phil Jamison. For openers, he has some good insights into the difference between bluegrass and old-time music:

"Bluegrass and old-time music are really very different. Old-time is more community oriented and participatory. It's intended for dance music. It's not performance music. Old-time music in concert can be quite boring, playing that same old fiddle tune over and over again. And sure, if the player is remarkable I can enjoy listening to it, but it's not intended for an audience. Its roots and tradition are all about dancing.

"Bluegrass developed as performance music with the advent of radio and recordings, and it was designed to grab the audience, to be entertaining. If I'm going to sit in a concert seat and listen to music, bluegrass is more entertaining than old-time. Players take solos as they would in jazz—they're flashy, they're showing their stuff—and as a result, it attracts that personality type who wants to be seen.

"I think shy people are more attracted to old-time music; I don't want to get out there and do the solos. I'd rather do the ensemble music. Part of the object of the old-time music is to not stand out. You want that ensemble sound where you're all chugging along and you don't want your instrument to stick out.

"Bluegrass is just the opposite. You want to feature each solo instrument, and when it's time for your banjo break to come, you want to stand out. That's why you put that resonator on so you can blast out and everyone can hear you.

"I do think they attract different types of people. I find the people who play bluegrass are maybe more competitive, or less shy, and old-time music is more about community by nature, and that's why it works so well at a place like this. I wouldn't say that as an absolute rule: There are certainly flashy people in old-time who want to show their stuff. It's just a general observation."

A Gathering of Kindred Spirits

Phil went on to describe the philosophy of this intimate and small event that draws 200 people a year.

"This program is called The Gathering because that's what it is—a gathering of musicians and a community, and that is very strongly felt. You can see it in the number of people who come here year after year, almost regardless of who's on staff. They come because there's so much happening outside of classes."

Phil thinks that about 50 to 60 percent of the people return every year, which just leaves 100 or so openings for new students. Phil doesn't want to expand The Gathering: "If you sell too many tickets, you sink the boat. Should it be bigger, or is it better to have a sense of community? You can't have a community with 500 people or 300. A couple hundred feels big to me."

I understand the attraction of community, but I wonder if this place, and banjo camps in general, can be an effective environment for people learning to play. Jamison has some concerns.

"We teach here, but we ourselves didn't learn this way. I taught myself. One person showed me how to do basic clawhammer; I read the Pete Seeger banjo book, listened to a lot of music, and basically figured it out myself. I never attended a banjo camp. I had a book of tablature that had banjo tunes in tab, and I also listened to some great clawhammer recordings from the Mount Airy/Galax area. But I had no way to slow the music down and had no way to transcribe. I just had to listen to it and try to figure out what was going on, note by note.

"One thing I find interesting, as a general rule, is that the people who teach here have never been students at places like this. What we're teaching, a school approach, breaking it down in that sort of way, isn't how we learned. But now that many of the artists and sources for this music are gone, the camps and resident summer programs may be the best way to pass along the aural traditions."

Plantation banjo player, c 1875

Dance Calling and the Banjo

"Dance calling comes from the African-American tradition of call and response, but that's something that has not yet been documented," Phil explains. "The banjo transformed British fiddle to create old-time music. The banjo is what really changed it. In the same way, African-American dance calling transformed British reels and cotillions to become the southern Appalachian square dance. Exact same process."

"Basically, when people from the British Isles came to this country, they played their jigs and reels. African-Americans picked up the fiddle as early as the 1600s and were playing for white people at dances. The combination of the British fiddle tradition and the African-American banjo coming together really created Appalachian old-time music. The banjo is what made the shift. Same thing with dance. The introduction of elements of African dance, specifically dance calling, transformed it to become the square dances that we have."

✹ THE NEXT GENERATION

With the Swannanoa Gathering in full swing, we can see and hear all this come together—first in Adam Hurt's class, transcribing and playing the work of Ed Haley, an old-time fiddler from West Virginia, and then at a post-luncheon concert that brings together legendary African-American fiddler Joe Thompson and the Carolina Chocolate Drops.

Adam Hurt ▶

Adam, only 23 years old, has already won wide critical acclaim and a Clifftop (West Virginia) first-place banjo title. With spiky black hair, wearing a T-shirt, jeans, and sandals, he was teaching a banjo version of a fiddle piece, "Poplar Bluff" (it's the first cut on his album, *Insight*). Hurt had translated the fiddling of Ed Haley, a blind musician—one of those latter-day Celts from West Virginia and East Kentucky, born in the 19th century—into contemporary clawhammer banjo. For the class, Hurt played a CD with Haley's original fiddle version to check the melodic line.

From his little boom box, through a cloud of hisses and cracks digitally mastered from an ancient wax-cylinder

recording, you could hear the wild fiddle of Ed Haley, seemingly off tune and riveting. Adam had to stop the piece several times to locate the melodic line and show how, for example, a double stop on the fiddle could be approximated by a banjo hammer-on attached to a Galax lick. The Galax or Round Peak lick is a rapid arpeggio on the bottom strings, ending on the 5th string (see Bob Carlin's workshop on page 94 for details).

CCD Concert

The Carolina Chocolate Drops concert, scheduled to take place at the Warren Wilson College gym, was already packed to near capacity when I arrived. The CCD are comprised of Rhiannon Giddens, an Oberlin-trained singer who refined her dance, fiddle, and banjo chops at past gatherings; Dom Flemons, an Arizona street musician and scholar who switches from bones to jug, to banjo, harmonica, and resophonic guitar with ease; and Justin Robinson, who comes from a classics and jazz background. They all sing and play multiple instruments.

Joe Thompson ▶

The concert is a CCD tribute to Joe Thompson. Thompson, an 88-year-old African-American fiddler, has been a key inspiration and mentor to the group. According to Rhiannon, The Chocolate Drops learned "Georgia Buck is Dead" from him, and he guided them into old-time fiddle music. Joe Thompson took center stage, playing fiddle and telling stories, backed up by the group. It was a performance that, like Adam Hurt's class, linked the past and present.

shindig ON THE green

Shindig on the Green

This tour of banjo camps ends, not with a camp at all, but a village green back in Asheville, called Martin Luther King Park. Open-air community jamming is what banjo camps are all about, and this place has got a long history of bringing together musicians.

Throughout the summer, "along about sundown," Shindig on the Green kicks off a summer evening of bluegrass and old-time music and dance. Performers start trickling onto the green in the afternoon and warm up in the jamming tents, while families stretch out blankets and keep an eye on the kids. Many people bring along folding chairs and make a big half-circle on the green around the stage.

No one knows in advance who will be performing, but with country musicians streaming in from all over Southern Appalachia, it's always a hoot. Coordinator Jackie Allison and her crew walk around auditioning groups and then build a performance list for the evening. Every group selected plays two selections, and there's some clog and smooth dancing onstage. There's a midway break during which everyone gets a chance to participate in something called a "chair dance," called by an MC.

Shindig on the Green grew out of the Mountain Music and Dance Festival started by Bascom Lamar Lundsford, the banjo-picking musicologist who did so much to preserve and spread traditional folk music. In the beginning, that festival was outdoors, and folks just naturally started jamming together off to the side, until it finally separated into its own thing.

Jammin' Tent
Pickers Only Please

The Mountain Dance & Folk Festival

The Mountain Dance & Folk Festival is a community event as well, only now it's indoors, tightly orchestrated, and you have to buy tickets and sit in theater seats to enjoy the likes of Bobby and the Blue Grass Tradition, Laura Boosinger, David Holt, along with storytellers and cloggers of all shapes and sizes. Shindig on the Green is outdoors in the park and is free of charge. Both events celebrate vintage roots. Come on over, y'all!

The Mountain Dance & Folk Festival and Shindig on the Green are both organized by an all-volunteer team in Asheville—the Folk Heritage Committee (info@ folkheritage.org, in case you'd like to get some advice on spreading music and dance around your town square).

A few weeks after Shindig closes down for the season, a relative newcomer—the Brewgrass Festival, a craft micro-brewery tasting event—takes over the park, and the music just keeps going. The featured act in 2007 was the Carolina Chocolate Drops.

BrewGrass Festival

Can't think of a better way to end this tour than to share one of the sights of all this music on the green, backed up by bluegrass and old-time banjos.

That's it for the tour. Now it's on to the old-time workshops. If you're just starting clawhammer banjo, Buddy suggests you begin with Ken Perlman's workshop. All old-time classes are held on the back porch of the Bait Shop, off Lonesome Pine Trail.

THE Ken Perlman WORKSHOP

INTRODUCTION

Banjo jokes are notoriously unfunny. A hangover from the minstrel area, they turn on the general incompetence of the banjo player. Two jokes come to mind to illustrate the economic life of a professional banjo player.

Question: *What is the difference between a mutual fund and a banjo player?*

Answer: One actually matures and earns money.

Question: *How can you tell the banjo player's car in the parking lot?*

Answer: By the Domino Pizza sign on the roof.

If you're single and living in the back seat of your salvaged Nash Rambler, making it as a banjo player may be as easy as taking to the streets with a five-string and an open instrument case to hold donations. For professional banjo players, thriving is no joke. It's a complex process that requires multiple talents—an accountant, manager, lawyer, and degree from Harvard Business School wouldn't hurt.

Pete Wernick, an early bluegrass picker, who hung around Greenwich Village as a kid picking up licks and riffs, emerged as a full-time industry with scores of books, videos, tapes, a performance schedule that could break the frequent-flier mileage bank, and a string

of music camps focused on bluegrass jamming. Bob Carlin performs, teaches workshops at banjo camps, and authors scholarly banjo books. Tony Trischka has best-selling songs on the bluegrass charts, books, CDs, a private teaching practice, national TV appearances, and leads workshops at banjo camps. Alan Munde has books, CDs, a touring band, a part-time job at banjo camps, and a job as a college professor. Jack Hatfield, Bobby Anderson, and Janet Davis own music stores. Et cetera.

And then there's Ken Perlman.

❋ A MAN OF MANY TALENTS

To call Ken a clawhammer banjo player is a bit like describing Bill Gates as a computer programmer. Perlman is one of the innovators of melodic clawhammer, which is something like putting the old frailing back-up rhythmic style on steroids and speed. Many of today's clawhammer banjo players taking lead breaks, playing close harmony, and performing solo are direct descendents of this work.

It's not just me saying this. *Frets* calls Ken a "clawhammer master." *Banjo Newsletter* says, "Ken is the undisputed king of the melodic clawhammer banjo style." I know this because he is savvy enough to put his accolades up on his website, which serves as central HQ for Perlman, Inc. It's all true. I've heard Ken play, and he's terrific. But that's just a piece of the pie. There's still a living to be earned, and like virtually every major banjo player, Ken has more irons in the fire than there are notes in an Earl Scruggs solo.

He performs, of course, frequently with fiddler Alan Jabbour, spending about one-third of his time on the road. He teaches privately and in banjo camps and workshops. He has several classic clawhammer instruction books and videos (and a few on fingerpicking guitar). Like many banjo players at Blue Mountain Banjo Camp, Ken writes a regular column for *Banjo Newsletter* but, unlike most, he's been doing it for more than 20 years. (His columns have been repackaged in book form and are available from Centerstream Music/Hal Leonard and Happy Traum's Homespun Tapes.)

Like Bob Carlin, Ken extends his range into academia. Under multiple grants, he has worked for a decade studying the fiddle music and folklore of Canada's Prince Edward Island, producing in the process a highly esteemed tune book (Mel Bay Publications), field recordings, and a two-CD set brought out by Rounder Records. With all of this, he continues to turn out well-reviewed performance CDs (you can check www.kenperlman.com if you really want the details).

But of all his multiple artistic, academic, and entrepreneurial achievements, nothing comes close to his role in creating banjo camps. For participating in Tennessee Banjo Institute, the very first banjo camp; co-coordinating the first independent, commercial camp; and spawning more camps than any other human in the Milky Way, Ken Perlman should be awarded the Golden Lanyard and Whistle award.

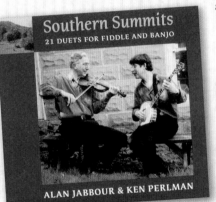

❖ HOW TO START A BANJO CAMP...

We met in Gatlinburg, Tennessee, in advance of the Smoky Mountain Banjo Academy program where Ken was to be the sole old-time instructor in a sea of bluegrass. In a series of conversations over that weekend—including one that took place during a nighttime drive as we searched, without success, for a good cup of coffee outside the commotion of camp— he traced the history of banjo camps for me.

"It all started with the Tennessee Banjo Institute. Three guys—rangers at a state park—decided to use some grant money. I can't remember right now, but I have their names written down. This was in 1988. A lot of other people were involved, like Hub Nitchie at *Banjo Newsletter*, and Eli Kauffman at the American Banjo Fraternity—these are guys devoted to late 19th century, five-string classic banjo."

Talking of the Maryland Banjo Academy, the first camp he managed in 1997, Ken said, "It was a big success. We made a lot of mistakes and learned. There were 150 or 200 people there, but it never occurred to us to organize the jams. You can get 20 fiddle players in a jam and they can work it out, but 20 banjo players without any melody is just chaos. Finally, one poor girl brought out a concertina she had with her. After that, we made sure we had at least one fiddle in every jam. There was one magical moment at that first camp: Pete Seeger came onstage, and the applause lasted 15 minutes before he played a note."

In Ken's workshop that follows, he takes clawhammer technique all the way back to the fundamental physical movements involved. Paying close attention can bring amazing results when you finally wrap yourself around an open-back banjo.

LESSON: AIR CLAWHAMMER

Hello. No reason to tune up right now. Getting people started who have never played clawhammer before has always proved a special challenge, particularly in the kinds of one-shot group settings that you encounter at banjo camps, other music camps, or festivals. Many times, you only have an hour or two to get people on a reasonable track towards learning, while at the same time inoculating them against crippling bad habits. And although it's not in the cards to hang around and see what they do afterwards, I still feel a responsibility for passing on advice that works.

I can't remember exactly how this developed, but a few years ago I hit on the idea of starting students out on the basic clawhammer motion without having a banjo in their hands. So first off, I'll advise you to put down your banjo, and follow this 10-step program:

Playing Air Banjo in Ken's 10-Step Program

Step One: Put the fingers of your right hand (RH) into a loose curve, and swing your forearm in towards your abdomen so your hand is close to your body. The palm should be facing the floor.

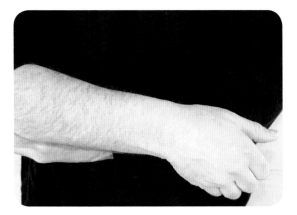

Step Two: *The natural arch.* The arch formed between hand and forearm should neither be pressed in, flat, or overly arched. The truly relaxed position (known as a *natural arch*) is where the top of the hand forms an ever-so-slight arch with the forearm, while the bottom of the hand and forearm—just by their construction—create the appearance of a more pronounced curve.

Step Three: *The floating wrist.* With the RH palm still facing the floor, take the index and middle fingers of the left hand (LH), and, with the LH palm facing up, place those two fingers directly under the wrist of the RH. Bounce your RH up and down a bit to get the feel of how the wrist should float.

Step Four: *Neutral position.* With the fingers of the RH still in a loose curve, rotate your right arm so that the palm is now facing the abdomen. Take your left hand and support your right-hand elbow. When the RH wrist is positioned straight off the arm, that's called *neutral position*.

Step Five: *The basic hand-motion.* Holding the arm as described in Step 4, move the RH wrist straight down, then return to neutral position. Do not bring your wrist past neutral position on the way up. Never allow your wrist to twist out of the vertical plane of motion.

Step Six: *Getting the forearm involved.* Try the basic motion again, but this time once the RH has reached its lowest point, allow the forearm to carry it a little bit further. Then as the RH returns to neutral, also carry the forearm back to the starting point. Be careful not to lose the curve of your RH fingers as you go through this maneuver.

Step Seven: *Applying Steps 5 and 6 to the banjo.* Now, take up the banjo and brace your upper forearm firmly on the armrest or rim. That acts as your pivot as you go through the stroke. Position your arm so that your RH is held over the strings in neutral position. Now, *without actually plucking any strings,* go through the motions described in Steps 5 and 6. In other words, move the RH wrist straight down, then return to neutral position. As the RH reaches its lowest point, allow the forearm to move with it. Then as the RH returns to neutral, the forearm carries it back to the starting point. Note that the forearm moves on the banjo by more or less "rolling" along the rim or armrest. (What actually happens is that the bottom or soft part of the forearm rolls, but the top part, where the bone is, remains virtually parallel to the banjo head.) This rolling is what transfers energy from the arm and shoulder to the downstroke.

Step Eight: *Selecting a picking finger.* About half the population are index finger users while the other half (including me) are middle finger users. Try both, and assume that a preference will establish itself within a week or two. Observe that the underside of the hand in clawhammer has all four fingers in a loose curve, with the picking finger slightly extended. All four fingers should be touching but not pressing together.

Step Nine: *The brush stroke.* With the hand held in a loose curve with one finger extended as described in Step 8, pluck the strings from 4 through 1, using the motion described in Step 7. The picking finger must be held relatively rigid to get sound out of the strings. Note that the hand as it moves across describes an arc, rather than a straight line. This is called a *brush stroke.* Make sure to let the thumb lag behind, so that the downward motion of the hand is stopped by the thumb being dragged into the 5th string.

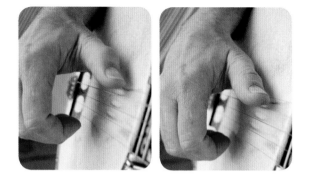

Step Ten: *The brush-thumb.* As you reach the bottom of your brush stroke and drag the thumb into the 5th string, you will feel a bit of tugging in the large joint of the thumb. Use that tugging to originate a thumb stroke, by slipping off the string and popping it at the same time. This is the way you transfer energy from downstroke to thumb stroke. This combined technique, called *brush-thumbing*, is the most basic movement of clawhammer. Now practice some brush-thumbs while changing simple chords, as shown in Exercise 1.

Once you master brush-thumbing, here's a seven-point program that gets you from there to where you can actually play music.

Beginning to Play with the 7-Point Program

Point One: *The single-string stroke on the first string.* Using just a small portion of the arc-like brush stroke, strike just the 1st string with the back of the fingernail. Try to avoid flicking the finger out to meet the string, and make sure to stiffen the picking finger sufficiently so that it provides resistance. Practice striking the strings while changing frets, as shown in Exercise 2.

Point Two: *The single-string stroke on strings 2–4.* When it comes to strings 2–4, there's a logistical problem in clawhammer that must be overcome: In short, how do you hit just one string without carrying other strings along with it. The best solution is to perform what is known as a *rest stroke*. In other words, after you strike a given long string, carry through so that the back of your fingernail rests ever so briefly on the next string directly in its path. For example, when you hit string 2, carry through so that the back of the fingernail rests ever so briefly on string 1. When you hit string 3, carry through so that the back of the fingernail rests every so briefly on string 2, etc. Performing rest strokes has the added advantage of making any given note project far better than would have otherwise been the case. Now practice striking all strings in turn, as shown in Exercise 3.

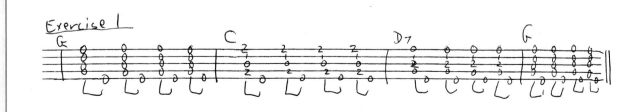

Point Three: *The bum-diddy strum.* The bum-diddy strum is the most basic way in clawhammer of filling up two beats in 4/4 time. It is made up of a single-string stroke followed by a brush-thumb. The timing is as follows: 1-_-2-&, 1-_-2-&, etc. There are actually four separate movements involved: Pluck, Recover, Brush, and Thumb. Here's how they work vs. the count. ▶ ▶ ▶

Observe that making "recovery" part of this routine tends to circumvent the almost universal tendency among beginners to rush the onset of the brush in bum-diddy maneuvers. Practice bum-diddy strums beginning on each of the banjo's long strings, as shown in Exercise 4.

• *Pluck* (strike) the string on count 1 with the back of the fingernail.
• *Recover* during the second half of count 1 (where an underscore appears). By "recover," I mean bring your right hand back into position where it can start the brush.
• *Brush* on count 2. As described in Step 9 on page 85, direct the picking finger arc-wise across the strings, and drag the thumb into the 5th string.
• Use the *Thumb* to play the 5th string during the second half of count 2 (where the "&" appears), as described in Step 10 (page 86).

POP IN YOUR CD NOW

Track 25: David Holt performing the bum-diddy

Point Four: *Skipping strings.* In Exercise 5, the order of long strings is changed to 1, 3, 2, 4. Notice that when you skip among strings like this, you either have to reach with your fingers (which changes the angle of attack) or shift the angle of your forearm relative to your upper arm. Shifting the forearm angle is the recommended method because it allows the angle of attack to remain constant as you move from string to string.

Point Five: *Finding a scale.* You can prepare to play tunes on the instrument by finding where the notes are. Start with a simple G-major scale in G tuning. First, hit each note twice in succession, as shown in Exercise 6a. Then, play each note just once, as shown in Exercise 6b.

Point Six: Integrate the G scale into a series of bum-diddy strums. Now, every time you play a scale note, follow it with a brush-thumb. In Exercise 7a, each scale note + brush-thumb is played twice. In Exercise 7b, each scale note + brush-thumb is played once.

Point Seven: Simulate playing a real tune by playing through Exercise 8, in which for three beats of a measure you follow the scale, and then fill in the fourth beat of the measure with a brush-thumb.

You are now ready to attempt your first tune. This arrangement of the old Appalachian classic "Water Bound" is a good one to get started with at this level.

Lots of luck in your playing!

Exercise 7a

Exercise 7b

Exercise 8

Water-Bound

THE Bob Carlin WORKSHOP

INTRODUCTION

When he walked onto the stage at Banjo Camp North's evening concert, it might have been the beginning of a vaudeville banjo act. Affable, wearing dark pink, teardrop-shaped, tinted glasses and a loud Hawaiian shirt, he exchanged a few jokes with the announcer, settled into a chair, tugged on his baseball cap, and tuned up. He smiled, sat up straight, and launched into a crisp, old-time tune, clawhammer style.

When the extended applause died down, Tony Trischka, the acknowledged dean of banjo, joined him for a laid-back, sophisticated musical conversation. That was my introduction to Bob Carlin, a banjo player in a class by himself in many ways. He could be a Renaissance man, if the Renaissance had record producers and talk show hosts. (Carlin produced more than 50 records and hosted WHYY's popular "Fresh Air" for years.)

One of the world's top clawhammer players (voted #1 for three years by readers of the prestigious magazine, *Frets*), Carlin is a serious world-class academic researcher and author. A New Jersey native, he is surely one of the foremost authorities in the Milky Way galaxy on North Carolina string bands and the origins of the American banjo. In addition to his scholarly books on the subject, the Bob Carlin collection of photographs, recordings, and research files—more than 13,000 items

covering the years 1824–2003—is archived at the famed Southern Folkways Collection at the University of North Carolina at Chapel Hill, right alongside the Mike Seeger and Alan Lomax collections.

And that's far from all of it. Carlin has four Rounder Records CDs and a Homespun instructional video, has authored banjo instruction manuals, writes a regular old-time banjo column for *Banjo Newsletter*, has published a ton of magazine banjo articles, and has toured extensively in the U.S., Europe, and Canada. And did I say he designed a popular old-time banjo produced and sold by Gold Tone?

To give you an even better idea of his reach, his two most recent duet albums are with his longtime music buddy, the late John Hartford, and Cheik Hamala Diabate, a distinguished West African ngoni performer. (The *ngoni*, kind of a stringed lute, is one of the contemporary banjo's ancestors.)

❖ A CAREER OF DIVERSITY

Next time I caught up with Carlin, we had lunch at the Mars Hill College cafeteria in Madison County, North Carolina. He was teaching at the Blue Ridge Old-Time Music Week meeting, a weeklong "camp" held on the campus. He was still wearing those glasses, a baseball cap, and his trademark Hawaiian shirt. He just didn't look like a clown anymore.

"So," I asked, repressing all questions related to costuming, "how do you account for the diversity of your career?"

"Survival. I think that has to come first," said Carlin, "and flexibility. All I have is a BA from Rutgers in radio-TV journalism, and I got a North Carolina grant to study banjo history. One motivation is to make a living within the larger venue of traditional banjo music. I just had to figure out how to have the skill sets I need. If radio is working, you go into that... or writing, or performing, or teaching. I'm pretty much a self-starter. So, if you need someone to go out and record and photograph while interviewing, and you ask me if I can do that, sure I can do that. And then I'd figure out how to do it.

"The other motivation is curiosity. I just want to know. I read way too much bad information about banjo history. I thought it would make my music better if I knew more about the history."

✺ SHARING THE LOVE OF OLD-TIME BANJO

I asked him why he was teaching at banjo camp.

"I'm friends with Hilary (Hilary Dirlam, the director)," Bob replied, "and she asked me to do this 10 years ago, and I was committed. Plus, it's a chance to hang out with old friends, and I'm just a couple of hours from home. Honestly it doesn't pay enough to justify doing it. I don't know why some people teach regularly at banjo camps. I would conjecture most could make more money elsewhere, unless maybe they don't have a gig for that weekend, or they see a chance to sell a huge amount of product or build an audience. (Dan) Levenson and I are doing our own traveling banjo academy where we go around the country and give intensive instruction in a weekend to 20 or 30 students. We've done it at Dusty Strings, a music store in Seattle, which already has classes going in their facility. We're doing a couple of others this fall.

"For camps, the real problem is educating people to pay high enough fees so instructor pay can be raised. In the music industry there's always someone who would do it cheaper...and most students can't tell the difference. In old-time music the problem is compounded because this music has always been semi-professionalized. That's what people like about old-time music. It's special to them; the whole world doesn't know about it, and they want it that way.

"It's very complex, this desire of people to keep it among themselves. (John) Hartford would say we don't want this music to get too big because then we'd have to share it with a whole lot of people we don't even like."

"And yet," I said, "here you are writing about old-time music, teaching it, performing, promoting your CDs."

"Right. I want everyone to know about this music, build a critical mass of demand. Beyond self-interest, we have to support the young, old-time bands that are out there. Right now, most of us 50-somethings who are performing are too young to be old farts and too old for young audiences to identify with."

It wasn't hard to understand what Carlin meant. Earning a living in the music business is tough. And it gets tougher as you move down the line. Lots of people know country stars like Garth Brooks and Doc Watson, and top echelon bluegrass performers like Earl Scruggs and J.D. Crowe can draw a crowd. How many old-time banjo players get their names up in lights? "I tell you true," said Jimmy Martin, the 'King of Bluegrass,' at the 1965 Roanoke Bluegrass Festival, "if we don't get no bigger crowds 'n this, how in the world we gon' get paid?"

I looked around the cafeteria where students were clearing their trays and heading out to jam sessions on the sunny lawns before the afternoon classes.

"It looks like there's a pretty good crowd right here at Mars Hill College, I said."

"I think this year," said Bob, "is the most successful program yet. You'll have to ask Hilary about that."

He thought a minute before going on. "But things are changing fast. Programs like these attract older adults and retired people, in general. We're in a transitional time for banjo instruction, moving into a different model, but we're not there yet. There are websites that offer online instruction, little bits and pieces. Another thing that's happening is the whole web cam thing, online direct instruction with a distant teacher.

"There is an undeniable surge in old-time banjo interest. Maybe it's the new, affordable high-quality, open-back banjos, or just renewed respect for traditional values in a world that seems to be losing its way."

✳ THE HISTORY OF THE BANJO

I saw Bob Carlin again a few weeks later as he performed his "History of the Banjo" mini-concert to a packed audience at a Malaprop's Bookstore reading in Asheville, North Carolina. His most compelling point seemed to be the way banjo fused African and European traditions—the banjo as the place where the British Isles meet West Africa, where rhythm and melody come together—the right hand African, the left European.

Over the course of an hour or so, he performed on a replica gourd banjo, a Civil War era fretless banjo, and the new signature Gold Tone. It wasn't an

unmanageable mob, but the manager had to bring out more folding chairs to accommodate the crowd. Sitting in the front row was a group of street musicians and a young kid with dreads halfway down his back.

Afterward, surrounded by an excited clutch of old-time groupies, Carlin signed a few books and sold a few copies of his recent CDs.

Wherever you fit into the continuum of folks who want to learn some good old-time Appalachian music, your Blue Mountain Banjo Camp old-time intermediate class instructor is Bob Carlin. So tune up and listen up. He's a classic.

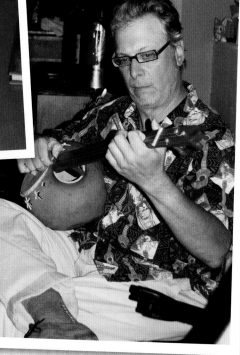

LESSON: TECHNIQUES & TUNES FROM MINSTREL BANJOISTS

Good morning. I'm going to teach a couple of songs in this workshop and then hand out tabs. For now, though, I just want to give you a little context for the tunes we're about to learn.

West African slaves brought banjo prototypes to the New World, in the process introducing early versions of the instrument into Anglo-American culture. From the study of West African musical instruments, it's obvious that the basic elements of banjo construction—the membranous soundboard and the short string played with the thumb—came from that area of the world. The right-hand, down-picking approach that was called "stroke" style in the 19th century and is known today by many names, including clawhammer, frailing, rapping, striking, and banging, to name a few, is also African in origin.

When this musical instrument, with its African rhythms and down-picking style, came to what was to become the United States, and players adopted the tunes and songs of European settlers, what emerged was a new and uniquely American musical form.

Besides descriptions published in period travel accounts and preserved in diaries and letters, there are few clues into the specifics of early playing styles and note choices before the advent of sound recordings in the late 19th century. Luckily, the first truly American form of popular entertainment, blackface minstrelsy, employed the banjo as an important part of its early history. From the early 1830s through the Civil War, banjoists accompanied singers and dancers, and formed the backbone of the freestanding minstrel ensembles that followed after the Virginia Minstrels of 1843.

Not all early minstrels had direct contact with African-Americans or came from the rural South. However, some southern banjoists (such as Virginian Joel Walker Sweeney) did bring aspects of black and southern influences into minstrelsy. Additionally, regardless of their origins, minstrel banjo styles had an effect on the subsequent generations of southern banjo players in their playing methods, repertoire, and banjo construction features through intensive touring by minstrels through the American South.

So, what were the techniques and tunes used by the minstrel banjoists that survive in southern old-time clawhammer banjo playing? Several early minstrel banjoists published books about their playing methods in the period around the Civil War, and these texts offer some clues and connections between minstrel and southern banjo styles.

If you have a pencil with you, you might want to make a note of some early sources. The five minstrel tutors I've gone back to in preparing for this class are: Briggs' Banjo Instructor (1855), Phil. Rice's *Correct Method for the Banjo: With or Without a Master* (1858), Howe's *New American Banjo School* (1859), Buckley's *New Banjo Book* (1860), Frank B. Converse's *Banjo Instructor Without a Master* (1865), and Frank B. Converse's *New and Complete Method for the Banjo* (1865). Most are available in facsimile reprint editions from Tuckahoe Music (P.O. Box 146, Bremo Bluff, VA 23022) or in tablature authored by Joseph Weidlich (Briggs, Converse, 1865), and in the compilation *The Early Minstrel Banjo*, published by Hal Leonard.

Some of the tunes presented in these minstrel instruction books that endure in southern fiddle and banjo music include "Dan Tucker," "Jordan Is a Hard Road," "Old Zip Coon," "Do, Mr. Booker, Do" (aka: "Johnny Booker"), "Darling Nelly Gray," "Devil's Dream," "Mrs. McCloud's Reel," "Sandy Boy," "Durang's Hornpipe," "Soldier's Joy," "The Celebrated Opera Reel," "Arkansas Traveler," "Fisher's Hornpipe," and "Money Musk Reel."

Minstrel Licks

The techniques I want to cover in this class are the *open string pull-off* and the *Galax lick* and *thumb lead*. I'll use two pieces to showcase these licks—the minstrel tune "John Diamond Walk Around" from the Rice book, and a modern North Carolina version of "Big Eyed Rabbit." OK, now you can tune up your banjos and let's see how it works.

OPEN STRING PULL-OFF

The open string pull-off is a left-hand technique. Instead of striking a string with your right hand that is either unfretted or fretted with the left hand, the left hand frets a note and then quickly pulls it off or plucks the string. The result is the sound of the open string. In minstrel banjo, this technique is often used on both the second and first string as the part of a melodic run, while in southern banjo playing, it's usually confined to the 1st string. Let's look at measure one of "John Diamond."

Working out of a C chord position (1st fret, 2nd string and 2nd fret, 1st string), the second note of the triplet (i.e. the 1st string) is pulled off from the 2nd fret to the open 1st string. This open string pull-off is used liberally throughout "John Diamond Walk Around," repeating the same figure in measures three, five and seven of the A part, and measures one, three, five, and seven (twice!) of the B part. The same open string pull-off is also found in measure four of part A.

"Big Eyed Rabbit" also uses the open string pull-off technique. In measure two of the A part, the 1st string is again pulled off with the left hand, here on the second and sixth eighth notes. Since I'm not working out of a chord position as in "John Diamond," I usually would pull off with the second finger of my left hand from the 2nd fret to the open 1st string.

GALAX LICK OR ROUND PEAK LICK

The Galax lick (or, as it more rightly should be called, the Round Peak lick), although associated these days with the North Carolina players Tommy Jarrell, Fred Cockerham, and Kyle Creed, is actually found throughout all southern banjo playing. It's also a feature of the minstrel instruction books, albeit using a different combination of right-hand fingers. The lick features, in its most basic form, an arpeggio across the 3rd/2nd/1st or just the 2nd/1st strings ending on the 5th string. Sometimes, a slide from the 2nd to the 5th fret of the 1st string is combined with the arpeggio.

In "John Diamond Walk Around," there are ancestors of the Galax lick in measures one, three, five, and seven of the A part, and in measures one, three, and five of the B part. Here, just the 2nd and 1st strings are sounded when leading up to the 5th string, with the 2nd sounded once, and the 1st sounded first as an open string pull-off and then as a fretted note. The more common minstrel version of the Galax lick leads with the open 3rd string, an open string pull-off on the 2nd string, the open 1st, and then the 5th. I've written this out as the "more common minstrel Galax lick." Ultimately, both versions occupy the same rhythmic space, with a triplet leading up to the plucked 5th string.

John Diamond Walk Around   G C G B D

more common minstrel Galax lick:

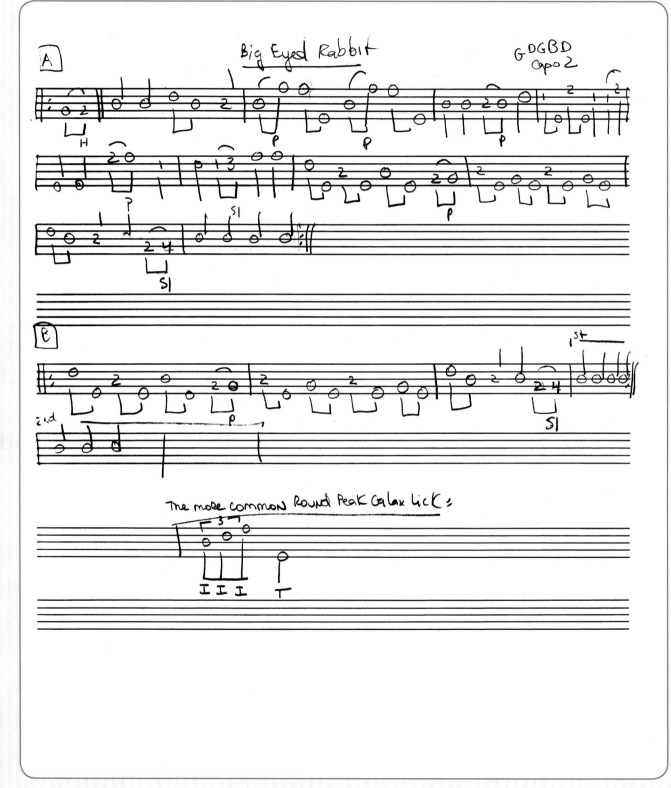

"Big Eyed Rabbit" has the more modern version of the Galax lick at the end of measure four leading into measure five. Here is the two-note/2-string variation, with two plucks of the 5th string rather than one. I've also written out the three-string version described above as the more common Round Peak Galax Lick.

Thumb lead is less common in today's southern playing, although Fred Cockerham does use a subtle version of the technique. It was extremely common in early minstrel banjo, as can be seen in "John Diamond Walk Around." Therein, the thumb is used prolifically at the beginning of phrases on the 2nd and 3rd strings, including starting the minstrel Galax lick. One finds faint echoes of thumb lead in the uses of the 5th string on the downbeat at the end of the Galax lick that begins measure five of the A part. A Fred Cockerham version of thumb lead occurs in the emphasis of the offbeat 5th string as if it were on the downbeat.

Hope that all works for you. You can pick up the tabs on your way out, but if you have any questions talk to me or send me an email: carlin@bobcarlinmusic.com.

You have a good day, now.

The Banjo Player, oil on canvas, Leon Delachaux, 1881

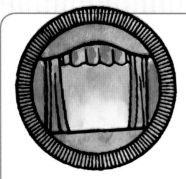

THE Music Hall Opera House

THREE-ACT SHOW

From the Grand Ole Opry in Nashville, Tennessee, to Radio City Music Hall in New York City's Rockefeller Center, the opera house/music hall has gladdened the hearts of audiences for centuries.

The music hall, originating in English taverns and bawdy houses during the early 19th century, offering song and comic routines, quickly made its way across the ocean to become American vaudeville and burlesque theatre. Unfortunately, serious lovers of classical music persisted in calling their auditoriums music halls as well, creating some confusion and no little animosity among revelers.

The opera house had similar difficulties in the beginning. Founded in the early 16th century, in Venice say some, in Florence say others, the opera house was designed to house productions of grand opera, much of which awaited the birth of Puccini and Verdi to be written. Giovanni DiCappella, a Venetian, is credited with the creation of this first opera house; however he was attacked by a Florentine rival and deprived of the instrument he was carrying—a kind of lute-like banjo precursor.

This unpleasantness was avoided in the Colonies as Americans fused the Music Hall and Opera House by virtue of an Appalachian colloquial pronunciation, creating the Opry House.

SHOW 1
GEORGIA BUCK IS DEAD
OR
Beginning Clawhammer
STARRING
David Holt

SHOW 2
THE HISTORY OF BANJO CAMP
Lecture and Slide Show

SHOW 3
BIG BEN
OR
It's All About You, Isn't It?
STARRING
Tony Trischka, Alan Munde, and Bill Evans

The Music Hall Opera House on Possum Trail offers entertainment certain to please!

Tickets are free to Blue Mountain Banjo Campers, but donations to the Blue Ridge Banjo Busker Association are always welcome. Please, no firearms allowed in the Opry House.

GEORGIA BUCK IS DEAD
OR
Beginning Clawhammer
STARRING
David Holt

The Cast

Brudder David Holt............the Teacher
Brudder Gomer Style.........the Student
Sister MaryLou...............Gomer's friend
The Chorus...................Tambo and Bones

The Actors

David Holt, a multiple Grammy award-winning musician, storyteller, and television host, has been deeply involved in the presentation and preservation of mountain roots music. A highly active performer, Holt tours with his band, David Holt and the Lightning Bolts, and often appears with Doc Watson at major bluegrass and mountain music festivals.

Gomer Style is the nom de theatre of Stomer Guile, a writer and aspiring banjo player who drifted into Blue Mountain Banjo Camp some months ago with a dream…and a book contract.

Sister MaryLou doesn't actually exist outside of a few lines in Act Three.

Tambo and Bones are two wandering minstrels who wanted to dress up as a Greek Chorus for this performance.

Act One

Prologue

(Tambo and Bones stand in front of the curtain.)

Chorus:
> This tale's construction
>> Is filled with instruction.
> So if you've come for entertainment
>> You'll have reason for complainment.
> Of drama there's none
>> Of laughter less, no clown
> No tears, no fun.
>> But there is something else instead:
> When the final curtain comes down
>> You'll know "Georgia Buck Is Dead"
> On your banjo, clawhammer style
>> Thus ending this play with a smile.

(They bow, trip over each other, and exit as the curtain rises.)

Scene One

(The scene is the courtyard of a mountaintop house deep in the woods. Arriving at David Holt's place for an interview, Gomer Style, a writer working on a banjo book, comes on stage loaded down with camera, tape recorders, and notebooks. David Holt, wearing a polo shirt, white Panama hat, and a broad smile, greets him at the door. They walk around a bit and then sit on the steps.)

GS: My first question: What do you call this kind of music?

DH: I call it old-time clawhammer music. I try for as many of the notes of the fiddle tune without losing the rhythmic drive of the tune. Of course, there are a number of styles inside old-time banjo. There's also the frailing or knocking style of clawhammer that focuses on a simple yet driving right hand and emphasizes the bum-diddy rhythm. There is also the Round Peak style, the style that came out of Surrey County, North Carolina.

GS: How would you characterize Surrey County style?

DH: You don't strum the chords but rather play lots of single notes. Lots of sliding. Very strong rhythmic right hand—it's not a bum-diddy, but a steady accented eight-note measure. It was originally developed on a fretless banjo, so now, even though we usually play fretted banjos, there's lots of sliding and it sounds like a fretless. I want to use what I learned from Tommy Jarrell and Fred Cockerham, other old-time fiddlers I knew when I was young, and apply it to the fancier mountain-style fiddle tunes people were playing up here in Asheville, North Carolina.

GS: Is there one overall name for all these styles?

DH: I call it mountain music. When I came to the southern mountains in 1969, there were all types of traditional old-time musicians, piano players, quirky three-finger banjo players, panpipe players, blues musicians, and lots of banjo and fiddle styles. In my mind, mountain music covers all types of music found in the mountains. Today it seems "old time" has come to mean banjo and fiddle tunes. The overarching term that would include everything that comes out of traditional music, including newly written songs, I'd call "roots music." OK, so how can I help you?

GS: I want to include a beginning clawhammer class in the book. Actually, how do you feel about teaching me the basics, from scratch, giving people a look at what it's like, one-on-one with David Holt? I'll take pictures, record the class, and put together a workshop. And maybe learn a song—say something like "Georgia Buck Is Dead."

DH: Sounds good to me. Want to do it now?

GS: Sure.

DH: Let me get my banjo. We can take some pictures while the light is still good.

(Lights dim, both exit stage. Curtain, end of Scene One.)

Scene Two

(David enters stage right, strumming a banjo. He shows Gomer which right-hand and left-hand shots he thinks he should photograph. They both walk over to the steps to start the lesson.)

DH: So…the clawhammer banjo is a combination of a drum and a melody instrument, and we're going to start with the rhythm part because rhythm is the most important thing in this style. It's not like three-finger (bluegrass) that's always changing; it's pretty consistent. And most people don't take the time to get the rhythm right. Let's just tap it on our leg. Bum/ did/dy Bum/ did/dy. This rhythm can be one two-and-three, rolling like that, or very exact.

*[**Author script note to director:** In* How to Play the Five-String Banjo, *Pete Seeger suggests a simple way to develop this syncopated rhythm. "Some find it easier to count 'one-two-three-four' very fast, and then keep silent on the 'two.' The resulting 'one…three-four' is the galloping banjo sound." This exercise is also on the Blue Mountain Banjo Camp CD, Track 25.]*

DH: OK, let's tap it out on our knee. Bum-diddy bum-diddy bum-diddy, bum-diddy. Good, that's what we really want. Very precise. Now partially close your right hand as if you were closing it around something about the size of a credit card in your palm. That's the claw position. Keep your fingers together. When you strike the strings, down, hit the string with your index fingernail. Try it. Relax your thumb a bit and let it be straight. There you go. Now, in any kind of music, we want the minimum amount of movement to get the maximum sound. Try it again with even less movement.

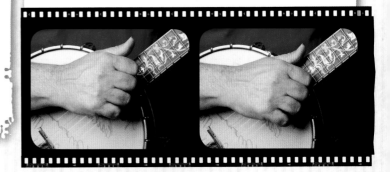

It's not all from your elbow; it's partly from your wrist. When you start going fast, you'll need that wrist action. Look at this. (*David plays rapid-fire clawhammer.*) See how my wrist is moving?

Next thing to pay attention to is where you strike the string along the fretboard. There are several places to get different sounds. Where the neck meets the head is usually pretty good, so let's try that and a few other places, like down by the bridge.

GS: Can I use the middle finger to strum instead of the index?

DH: You know what, I started out with my middle finger and it works fine. It produces a little bit of a warmer tone. I use both, to tell you the truth, as background to my singing, but most people don't do that. They just choose one finger to use. Your middle finger is OK. But the index finger produces the strongest sound.

GS: Right. Now it's just in the way…

DH: If it's in the way, just turn your hand a bit so the little finger moves away from the banjo head, and slow down because precision is a lot more important than speed. Like any folk instrument, clawhammer banjo was designed for hardworking people who didn't have a lot of time. Maybe they could pick it up for a few minutes after coming in from the fields in the evening or while sitting on the porch before going to bed. It's the kind of thing you can do five minutes a couple of times a day. You can even do it watching TV, just so long as

you don't drive people crazy…maybe five minutes five times a day. Just do it slow. Now, let's tune up and start playing.

(*They tune to a G chord—DGBD, counting from the top, or the short 5th string down—using one of those little clip-on electronic gadgets.*)

DH: OK, we're going to strike the 1st string and the 5th string. What we're looking for is an even tone. You want all notes to have the same volume. Now try striking the third string with your index fingernail; come back to the closed position, then strike the 1st string with your index finger, and then, with your thumb, hit the 5th string, keeping the bum-diddy rhythm.

Let me point something out. It's starting to sound good, but your beats are all the same. There is an accent on the 2nd and 4th beats. It's subtle, but put a little more power on those beats. For now, just do it on one string (no brush) so you can feel it better—BUM (third string) DID (first string) DY (fifth string).

(*They do it together for a few minutes as the lights dim and the curtain falls. End of Scene Two.*)

Scene Three

(*The curtain rises on the two men seated on the steps. David is examining Gomer's thumb.*)

DH: You might try striking the 5th string over here, at the edge. You have a little more control here because you have that ridge before the fleshy bump of the thumb.

(*David marks the ridge for Gomer with a ballpoint pen. Gomer starts strumming.*)

GS: Feels different.

DH: Stronger. OK, that's pretty nice. Now, let's get a little more precise with the 5th string. Your thumb gets cocked pretty much like you're doing. Don't make it tense on your thumb in any way. Does that feel uncomfortable? Try to catch it on your thumb groove. Good.

Now, to make it more interesting, we're going to add the brush strum. Hit the 3rd string, and then brush on the 3rd, 2nd, and 1st strings in the same amount of time. And then pluck the 5th string with your thumb.

Hit the 3rd string—BUM—brush the bottom three strings—DID—and pluck the 5th string—DY. Good, now slow down a little bit.

GS: My thumb is wandering all over the place.

DH: If your thumb spazzes out, that's going to happen. Just do it every day and, in two or three days, it will stop doing it.

Let's practice switching bass strings between the G (3rd string) and the B (2nd string). Strike the 3rd string, (BUM), brush on bottom three (DID), 5th string (DY), and then the 4th string (BUM), and brush on first three (DID), and 5th (DY). The thumb stays resting on the 5th string. Good. Keep going. For this next week, I want you to do this a thousand times, five minutes at a time, five times a day. It seems incredibly boring, but just look at it as a little meditation. See how long you can do it without blowing it. (There are dozens of repetitions of this as David plays along with Gomer. As the repetitions keep rolling on, the rhythm takes over, strong and booming. It sounds like old-time banjo!)

(*Curtain falls, end of Act One.*)

Act Two

Scene One

(The curtain rises on a room filled with banjos and guitars. Gomer and David are sitting on chairs across from each other. There is a computer, sound equipment, and performance posters on the wall. David is wearing a baseball cap.)

DH: Do you know the G, D, and D7 chords?

GS: I do, but my right hand index finger isn't picking out the strings accurately.

DH: Your fingers are all getting choked in there because your hand is not turned away from the head. Good, that's it. And watch the rhythm. What I want you to do is make it almost a dotted note, thumb really snapping in there at the end. This bum-diddy is the very basic building block. Practice it along with the CD we'll make for the book.

The tricky thing about clawhammer is you're working with muscles on the back of the hand, but they never do anything else. So look at this (makes slight up and down movement of wrist). This is the kind of motion they have to make. It's a very miniscule motion. Here is another exercise to help develop control.

Our first exercise is to play two bum-diddies on each string, and then go on to the next string so it sounds like this: Listen. (He plays.) Two bum-diddies on each string. That is, BUM on the 1st string, recover, and strike the DID on the same 1st string, and follow that with the DY on the 5th string.

GS: I'll give it a shot.

(Gomer repeats the exercise for a seemingly excruciating amount of time, and David—trained professional, TV personality, and all-around nice guy—continues to be pleasant and patient.)

DH: OK, that's great…excellent. Good, 2nd string, great, 1st string, 2nd string, 3rd, 4th, now back down again to the 3rd, the 2nd. If it starts to drive you crazy, deaden the strings. (He lightly places his left-hand fingers on his fret board, muffling the sound, and continues the exercise with his right.) Now, let's go back to the strumming stroke, the brush stroke, and see if we can change chords.

GS: This is harder than it looks…

DH: Keep your fingers close to the fret, right behind the fret. (Still patient…unbelievably so.) Here's what's happening, Gomer, my friend. You're moving ahead too fast because you're starting to hear music. We're going to slow it down. They play at about one bum-diddy every two seconds.)

GS: This is not going all that well.

(Curtain closes to a chorus of slow bum-diddies; it should sound discouraged, played decrescendo.)

Scene Two

(Same set)

DH: Let's go back to the exercise where we do two bum-diddies on each string.

(Gomer plays, struggling to slide his fingers up to the frets.)

DH: That's good, that's very accurate. Great. Do you think you'll be able to take some time to keep it slow? Most people can't, they have to start speeding up, adding the music. I can pretty much promise you, guarantee, if you keep doing this exercise you'll have a much stronger right hand, and the left hand will take care of itself.

I've got this written out for you. See, look at this tab. Start with your index finger on the 1st string, thumb on the 5th. Practice the brush stroke, and once you feel really comfortable, add the chords, and then practice that thing going down one string to the next.

There's no need to sit down and do this for hours. Actually, sitting down for five minutes, and then, two hours later, another five minutes is best. It's teaching muscle memory, and that doesn't come in one long session, but in many short sessions. Basically, practice by doing the bum-diddy, then add the brush stroke across the three bottom strings, and finally add chords when you get bored out of your skull.

Let's get together next Monday. A week is about right to check up on progress and move ahead. And, if you're ready, we'll move on to "Georgia Buck."

GS: OK, see you then.

(Curtain. End of Act Two.)

Act Three

Scene One

(Curtain rises on the interior of Gomer's trailer. MaryLou, his girlfriend, is sitting on the edge of the bed, smoking.)

ML: I don't see the big deal. All you're doing is going up to David's to learn that dumb song you've been practicing.

GS: It's not dumb, and I haven't been practicing it. I never learned it. All I'm practicing are exercises. Exercises. This is "Georgia Buck Is Dead." A classic. David recorded it. Rhiannon sang it on the Chocolate Drop's CD. Joe Thompson played it at the Swannanoa Gathering. Can't you see? Now it's my turn!

(He sits down beside her on the bed, his head in his hands. She puts her arm around him.)

ML: Gome, it will be all right. How hard can it be if all those guys play it?

GS: Hard? It's not hard. That's the point. It's such a basic song—four-four time, three chords in the key of G. Could be a million blues and old-time songs—that's why I can't blow it.

(From outside the trailer, the Tambo and Bones Chorus starts singing, first low and mournfully then upbeat, louder.)

> *Georgia Buck is dead*
> *And the last words he said*
> *Don't put no shortenin' in my bread*
> *Don't put no shortenin' in my bread.*
> *O, no. O, no.*
> *Don't put no shortenin' in my bread*

ML: Now what the hell does that mean? Of all the things to go through the mind of a dying man—don't put no damned shortening in my bread?

(The Tambo and Bones Chorus starts a rousing gospel-like version of "Mama's Li'l Baby Loves Shortnin' Bread.")

> *Mama's little babies love shortnin' shortnin';*
> *Mama's little babies love shortnin' bread*
> *When those children, sick in bed*
> *Heard that talk 'bout shortnin' bread*
> *Popped up well to dance and sing*
> *Skipped round and cut the pigeon wing.*

ML: Maybe Georgie Buck had enough of cornbread and beans and misery and just didn't want to pop up to dance and sing no more.

(ML and GS look at each other and shrug. Curtain.)

Scene Two

(Curtain rises on David Holt's studio. The tablature for "Georgia Buck is Dead" [see page 106] takes up the entire back wall of the set. David and Gomer are sitting opposite each other in the studio, as before. Each has a banjo.)

DH: Let's go back to the little licks we were doing, because it's all going to fit together in the song in a few minutes. You're going to hammer on from the 2nd fret to the 4th fret.

GS: I'm switching to my index finger to start the hammer-on.

DH: Definitely. Index finger and hammer down with the ring finger. Now do it again. Second fret third string, hammer-on to the 4th fret, now back to the 2nd fret, and pull-off. When you pull-off, pull down on the string to snap it, and bring the index finger back onto the 2nd fret 2nd string, which will start the final bum-diddy of measure two. Try that a couple of times. Good, that's the sweet spot on the banjo right there.

GS: The hammer-on and pull-off equals one bum-diddy.

DH: Right. Just do it real slow, so slow you can actually think through each thing you have to do. And when you pull-off, remember to snap the string and actually rest your thumb on the 5th string. Don't push on it—just very lightly rest it.

Now, let's try the slide we were working on. Middle finger on the 3rd string, 2nd fret, and slide up to the 4th string and brush. The slide is done during the bum beat of the bum-diddy. Good, now I think we can put them together and play a tune or do them as an exercise. Here's how it goes. *(David plays and sings.)* OK, now you try it.

(Gomer plays it.)

DH: Good, but you have to hold your finger closer to the fret and really pull off. One reason that's important is you have so many hammer-ons and pull-offs to get those fancy notes, you have to practice to get them all at the same volume as the notes you actually strike. A person not indoctrinated into this stuff wouldn't know how I'm getting all these notes. Let's play it through together one time.

(They play.)

"Georgia Buck Is Dead" Trad. Arr. By David Holt
High Windy Songs, BMI

My name is Georgia Buck
Never had no luck
Always been treated this away, boys
Always been treated this away
I said, "Oh, me. Oh, Lordy my,
Always been treated this away."

Cornbread and beans
Is all I've ever seen
Ain't gonna be treated this away, boys
Ain't gonna be treated this away
I said, "Oh, me. Oh, Lordy my,
Ain't gonna be treated this away."

Got nothing left to show
For all this traveling down the road
Guess I'll just up and travel on, boys
Guess I'll just up and travel on
I said, "Oh, me. Oh, Lordy my
Guess I'll just up and travel on

Georgia Buck is dead
And the last words he said
Were, "Don't put no shortin' in my bread, boys
Don't put no shortin' in my bread
I said, "Oh, me. Oh, Lordy my.
Don't put no shortin' in my bread."

Georgia Buck is dead
And the very last words he said
Were, "Dig me a hole in the ground, boys
Dig me a hole in the ground"
I said, "Oh, me. Oh, Lordy my.
Dig me a hole in the ground."

DH: Isn't that nice? To me, it's the best use of four notes anybody has done, and it leads right into "Georgia Buck."

GS: It's easier if I slide, holding the note down with my left-hand index finger.

DH: You might as well get used to using your middle finger. In your life as a banjo player, you'll slide a thousand times with this finger, ten thousand times, so go ahead and use it. Slide up on the middle finger, then switch to your index finger for the hammer-on in the second measure. Ready for "Georgia Buck?" OK, but we're going to go slow. The reason I keep harping on this is everyone wants to play fast to see what it sounds like. If you learn it wrong it takes two times as long to learn it right

GS: Cool.

DH: You probably know this already, but when you have a little spot that is a problem, use it as an exercise. Work on it until you can slug it into the song at the fastest speed you can handle, and put something before and after at the same speed, like building one of these little Lego things. Now let's move on to "Georgia Buck."

Now, when you start the slide in the first measure—see, that's the same slide we've been working on—don't start way back here. Move closer to the fret. It will save you a little energy, and sound better. And don't hammer on until you get up to the note. OK, try it.

(Gomer plays it and messes up.)

DH: Relax. Let's take it from the beginning, slow. This time, start from here, at the pickup.

DH: All right! Play it by yourself one more time; start with the pickup and play it close to the frets.

GS: I'm playing "Georgia Buck Is Dead." And it doesn't completely suck.

DH: Here, let me get the whole thing on tape for you.

Track 26: David Holt plays "Georgia Buck Is Dead"

(Gomer, exuberantly pleased with himself, plays as lights dim.)

(Final curtain.)

(Tambo and Bones walk out in front of the curtain in tuxedo and top hat.)

> This workshop ends, as you can see.
>> But its lessons you'll find on your CD.
> Just take a look
>> In the back of the book.

(They bow, and exit, stage left. All lights go out. In the darkness, a quiet thrum of banjo music can still be heard.)

The End

THE HISTORY OF BANJO CAMP
Lecture and Slide Show

A Brief Review of the Banjo's Colorful Origins

Before there were banjo camps, there was—the banjo! Listen to old-time banjo and you'll hear the steady loping thrum of an African drum, the courtship song of a plantation slave, the Appalachian retelling of a history tale, a lament, a love song—all in the bright and resonant voice of the banjo.

Survivor of hardship and thievery—traveling to the Americas in the stinking holds of slave ships crashing across oceans, strapped to the backs of settlers and soldiers slogging across mountains, and cowboys on roundup—the banjo is the ultimate American instrument. Loud, pushy, insistent, plaintive, optimistic, and filled with wild energy, the five-string banjo, wherever manufactured, is uniquely made in America.

African born, surely, with likely Middle Eastern and Asian forbears, but the banjo is America's own instrument. The cheerful consolation of the driven African slave working Southern cotton fields, and the unfailing companion of the Appalachian family working hard land in isolated mountain valleys, and the solitary homesteader on the great prairies, the banjo quickly spread throughout the boisterous, expanding American culture. From minstrel shows and county fairs to gospel choirs, church meetings, picnics, and simple get-togethers, Americans just naturally came to work, play, and courtship with banjos on their knee.

African-American musicians in a minstrel line, c. 1860s. Courtesy Jim Bollman

108

Fretted instrument ensemble, c. 1896. Courtesy Jim Bollman

What could be more melting-pot American than fitting a fretted European fingerboard to an African gourd to create a music-making instrument that gives strident voice to the hopes and fears of the common man and woman? You can't get much simpler than a pole stuck in a hollow gourd strung with gut or twine. And the first handmade banjos in America, beefing up the pot by replacing the calabash gourd with one made of wood, barely improved on that design.

When America's antebellum aristocrats, young European plantation kids for the most part, would listen to the African rhythms, the sound of the banjo and dancing coming from the dark slave shacks, they took the songs and the instrument for their own. Some, in the 1840s, brought the banjo onto the stages and workplaces of the industrial North.

For two decades, until the Great War Between the States broke out, minstrelsy resulted in improved banjo design, expansion of the repertoire, and the spreading of the gospel of the banjo in both the New and Old Worlds.

✹ AFTER THE CIVIL WAR

The next wave of banjo evolution had to wait until America recovered from the War Between the States. The blending of cultures resulting from that war and the rising popularity of minstrelsy created expanded interest in the banjo and rapid development of better-made instruments. The 20th century opened with a double boost for the banjo. The sharp syncopation of banjo rhythm, translated to piano by its greatest innovator, Scott Joplin, contributed to the ragged rhythms that took over a nation. In addition to ragtime, out of New Orleans came the marching Dixieland bands and the birth of swing, contributing to a four-string tenor and plectrum banjo craze.

In Appalachia, five-string banjo continued to dominate, and this strain of Irish, Celtic, English, and Welsh folk music morphed into the American canon of old-time, country, and hillbilly classics before branching off into bluegrass.

Rural family stringband, c. 1900. Courtesy Jim Bollman

✿ PUSHING THE BANJO BOUNDARIES

Two names stand out in the next evolution of the banjo in the mid-20th century. For bluegrass, it's Earl Scruggs, the electrifying three-finger picker who first gained recognition with Bill Monroe and the Blue Grass Boys on the Grand Ole Opry stage in 1945. Scruggs supplied the distinctive rapid-fire lead banjo breaks and the strong banjo rhythmic backup that would become the hallmark of this music.

In the tradition of old-time and folk music, at the same time, Pete Seeger created new songs and popularized the five-string banjo in the folk revolution he helped bring about through his singing, books, television show, and public appearances.

The boundaries are still being pushed. At the opening of the 21st century, musicians like Tony Trischka, Bela Fleck, and Pete Wernick are exploring new musical directions, fusing classical, jazz, and world music on basically the same humble, round-faced banjo that surfaced in America in a plantation shack more than 300 years ago.

✻ AFTER WORLD WAR II

The infant electronic industry that emerged from the Second World War brought with it data processing, mass communications technologies, and dramatic cultural changes. As America flexed its post-war muscle and its great industries exploded, Highway 66 was replaced by interstate highways that crisscrossed the continent, linked cities, and displaced villages and small towns. TVs and computers moved to the center of American life, and stable families and whole communities started to break up as rich and restless Americans altered their priorities, and searched for better jobs, better housing, and better schools.

By the time we looked up, the music had stopped.

From being creators of music, we became a nation of consumers. Instead of making music together, we were buying it, alone, and listening to it on the radio and CD players. Soon, a growing reaction to the loss of traditional music led to intensive fieldwork and field recordings, and renewed interest in old-time and folk music done by people like Alan Lomax and Mike Seeger.

The Birth of Banjo Camps

It's in this environment—this time of rapid change and clashing cultures, of outdoor three-day bluegrass festivals and wildly popular folk festivals, all of which attracted tailgate jammers and hootenannies—that banjo camps were born.

❊ TENNESSEE BANJO INSTITUTE STARTS IT ALL

The first formal banjo camp, however—the Tennessee Banjo Institute—wasn't held until 1988. Tennessee state park ranger Wayne "Buddy" Ingram and park interpretative specialist Bobby Fulcher, both banjo enthusiasts, organized TBI, which was held in Cedars of Lebanon State Park, in Lebanon, Tennessee. "There had been gatherings before," said Ingram, "but nothing of that magnitude. People came from Europe and Africa to participate," Bobby explained.

It all started when Wayne Ingram wanted to host a workshop with classic, bluegrass, old-time, and minstrel music. Ingram's interest had been primarily bluegrass until he was introduced to old-time minstrelsy banjo. Bobby Fulcher, who had organized some 20 music festivals for the park system all over Tennessee, and worked on a few national events, believed Wayne's idea could become a festival, rather than a workshop. Once the concept was approved, he "worked night and day" on the project, getting funding and lining up teachers and supporters. Wayne spent the bulk of his workday organizing park facilities and administrative support for TBI.

1992 Tennessee Banjo Institute

Cedars of Lebanon State Park

Classes were held in Old Cedar Forest Lodge, a WPA structure built in the '30s, as well as the park recreation building, small cabins, and temporary shelters. "The banjo world," said Fulcher, "learned more about itself during that three-day period than it had through any other means outside of *Banjo Newsletter*. At TBI people had to look at each other, see the Africans and minstrel style, the gourd banjos. As far as I know the first presentation of griots and their banjo-like lutes to the banjo community was at TBI. At that first camp, there were 35 teachers and 120 campers, called 'members' of TBI."

The Importance of the *Banjo Newsletter*

The support of *BNL* editor/publisher Hub Nitchie (seen here) and his wife Nancy was critical to the success of this first camp and, in a sense, all others. "The *Banjo Newsletter* was a big inspiration to me and to Buddy," said Bobby. "Here was *BNL*, an institution in itself, that valued the diversity of banjo music and was open-minded about the banjo's role musically and open to exploring its place in history. We just adopted that approach to the TBI."

The stamp of TBI is on every ensuing banjo camp. The TBI schedule format, maps, manufacturers' sponsorship, and program organization are nearly identical to those found in banjo camps 20 years later. Their efforts were extraordinary. "It was amazing," said Nancy, "because Buddy and Bobby managed to bring an entire mento band up from Jamaica. The mento are 'Barbaries'—slaves who had escaped from slavery in the early 1800s and lived in little settlements in the mountains without electricity or schools."

Hub Nitchie died of complications from surgery shortly before the third, and last, Tennessee Banjo Institute session in November, 1992. As a memorial to Hub, Nancy called on Jack Hatfield and Ken Perlman, both contributors to *BNL*, to organize the Maryland Banjo Academy.

"Jack and I got together," said clawhammer banjoist and author Ken Perlman," and contacted mostly *BNL* teachers and columnists. I did the old-time banjo planning and Jack did bluegrass. The first Maryland

Banjo Academy camp was in 1997. MBA ran every 18 months. There were three camps all together, and then *BNL* took a break for a couple of years."

☼ MORE CAMPS EMERGE

During the two-year interval after the third camp, in the summer of 2002, other camps sprang up, the first major one being Banjo Camp North in Groton, Massachusetts, started by Mike Holmes and Ken Perlman. That first Banjo Camp North drew more than 200 participants, mostly from the Northeast. After Ken and Mike split up—don't ask—Ken went on to organize other banjo camps around the country: Midwest Banjo Camp, American Banjo Camp, and Suwannee Banjo Camp.

Independent banjo camps were by no means the only resident programs teaching banjo. John C. Campbell was doing it in the 1920s, including instruction for an all-woman banjo band. For 50 years, Chicago's Old Town School of Folk Music has been offering banjo instruction on a grand scale. More than 6,000 students weekly study various folk instruments at this institution, which has been sponsoring the

Chicago Folk and Roots Festival since 1998. In 1978, Warren Wilson College in Swannanoa, North Carolina, started its Appalachian Studies programs that included instrument training. But the sheer intensity and concentration on a single instrument in all its forms make banjo camps unique.

As a means of overcoming the depersonalization of a media-saturated, technological society, you couldn't ask for a better in-your-face, up-close-and-personal, musical experience, complete with mud and mosquitoes and all the community you could ever ask for.

Banjo instruction is included in other resident music camps—both college-based and independent. Some of these camps are simply called "jam camps" or "acoustic camps," and fold banjo instruction into a matrix of other bluegrass, folk, and old-time music instruction. Camps such as these hark back more to the earlier days of Bean Blossom and High Point tailgate festivals, where folks pulled up in trailers and pickup trucks, set up tents, and listened to acts like the Stanley Brothers, Bill Monroe and the Blue Grass Boys, Earl Scruggs and the Foggy Mountain Boys, the Osborne Brothers, J.D. Crowe, and between acts—and all night long—would jam together, exchanging songs and licks.

Banjo camps, through innovations like slow jams, and in their focus on building rhythm, backup, and lead skills to permit banjoists to jam, have contributed to the regrowth of community. Playing banjo is rarely a solo proposition. The banjo comes into its own when joined by a fiddle scraping out double stops, a thumping bass, guitar, mandolin, Dobro, washboard, whistle, or voices raised in song. For nearly 300 years, that's the way Americans made music together.

Camps are continuing to evolve, spreading across the country, adding features and amenities. Some, like the Sonny Osborne and Bill Evans' Nash Camp, are known for cuisine as well as bluegrass. Some are huge affairs. But all of today's banjo camps keep other musicians around—bass players and fiddlers, guitarists and mandolinists—to keep the banjo company. (Actually, that's a banjo joke.)

Campfire CONVERSATIONS

What do you do with all the good stories and snapshots that just don't fit on the Bluegrass Express and Old-Time Horse & Buggy Tour, and aren't exactly workshops? We don't want you to walk away from Blue Mountain Banjo Camp without getting a chance to visit with these folks a bit, so we set up a campfire to share some of this with you. You've got to supply the logs, pinecones, marshmallows, and any other refreshments. At the very least, you'll come away with some new perspectives.

For example, Tony Trischka has a wicked sense of humor. Even before he walked away with the three top International Bluegrass Music Association awards in 2007, he was a bigger-than-life figure in the banjo world. An informal campfire conversation should help round out your picture of him.

Janet Davis, one of the most rigorous and formidable banjo teachers in print, turns out to be a totally different person close-up.

And then there's Wayne Erbsen, mostly known for his *Ignoramus* banjo books. What kind of banjo did this serious academic and best-selling author bring to the campfire?

Chances are you don't know John Herrmann unless you're an old-time aficionado. Pull a stool over to the fire and listen up. His insights from his life as a busker and his opinions on traditional music make for good listening.

The legendary Bill Keith, one of the few players who bridge the great divide between Earl Scruggs and Bill Monroe, shares his recollections of the early days.

And Brad Leftwich, the quintessential old-time fiddler and banjo player, is hunkered around the fire with some insights on really hearing music.

Finally, there's Pete Seeger, to whom this camp is dedicated. Some of his stories—like his near accident when his mother had a big pot boiling on an open fire ready to wash his diapers—well, they just don't fit into the book. But while sitting around this campfire, strumming and picking banjos, anything goes. And, admit it, doesn't it warm your heart to think of little Pete Seeger in diapers?

Anyway, we've got the photos and stories, conversations, and opinions. Got a match?

Buddy McCoy

Tony Trischka
HIMSELF

It was a Saturday morning class taught at the Meeting Room, a white building up the hill a bit from the waterlogged Baptist camp that housed Banjo Camp North. This was the class I registered for months ago, or at least the teacher I came to see.

In all my driving around East Coast banjo camps, the CD that kept me company was Tony Trischka's *Double Banjo Bluegrass Spectacular*. If you don't already have it, even if you have to hock your original 78-RPM *Flatt & Scruggs at Carnegie Hall* album, get it. It will wake up your ears to the range of bluegrass music possible from the five-string banjo in the hands of master musicians. Having risen to the top of the national bluegrass charts and walked away with the IBMA Album of the Year, the CD has had a powerful influence on bluegrass and five-string banjo.

Behind the CD is Tony Trischka, a big, shambling, bear-like guy, with a dry, New York sense of humor that punctuates his onstage performances and classroom sessions. Wearing a beat-up shapeless sweater, jeans, and muddy running shoes, he lets you know right off he's not obsessed by glitz. In performance and around camp, he's relaxed, accessible, talking, ideas stumbling over one another, always moving on to the next thing, until he picks up his banjo. Typically, even when he plays small exercises demonstrating, say, sixth intervals, you'll hear clarity of execution, precision timing, and an unbounded ferocious musicality.

GS: Where are you from?

TT: Syracuse. I was brought up there. My father was a physics professor. And he played musical instruments.

GS: What kind of name is Trischka?

TT: Czech. My great-grandfather was a wallpaper designer and emigrated to Germany.

GS: And you're married?

TT: Yes, living in New Jersey, two kids: Sean, 13, a drummer, and Zoe, 10. She's a dancer.

GS: So touring must be tough on the family.

TT: It's gotten better. Now I do only 80 or 100 dates a year. I used to be gone six weeks at a stretch. With the success of my album and a new bluegrass band, I'm around more.

GS: When is your next CD coming out?

TT: Smithsonian Folkways is bringing out a CD. They finished mastering it. It was originally intended to be a dozen solo tunes. Now it's six solos and then six songs that were going to be on the Double Band. Rounder thought they weren't bluegrass. Mike Seeger and Pete

Seeger and Bill Keith are on them and they weren't really bluegrass, more folk. So those are on there, along with Bill Evans.

GS: What are you excited about musically these days?

TT: If I have a really good gig, that could be exciting. And I'm writing a new fox-hunt tune. I saw a video from the '50s with DeFord Bailey, an African-American harmonica player, the first black on the Opry, playing a fox hunt and thought, "I want to do something on the banjo like that."

GS: What do you think about the musical limitations of the banjo and the limitations of the bluegrass form?

TT: Depends on musical personality. Earl Scruggs just plays his style, constantly changing in subtle ways. Someone like him is happy playing that. I asked him about melodic style, and he said it just doesn't fit his roll. Some people are happy and don't hear anything else. Others, like Scott Vestal, I heard him with Doyle Lawson, and went to a hotel room to pick and started jamming. He started doing some of the Bela (Fleck) stuff.

I asked him if Doyle knew he was doing this, and he said no. "I like the straight ahead stuff, but I hear other sounds as well."

I grew up listening to jazz, rock-and-roll, and classical music. I look at the banjo as a complete musical instrument. The very first thing I played on my first banjo, a Christy long neck, was Beethoven's "Ode to Joy." Now, bluegrass is what's coming out. For my 18th anniversary, I'm trying to write a tune in three groups of 6/8 time—a dueling banjo tune.

GS: What about teaching methods?

TT: Anyone I start teaching from scratch, I'll show him "Boil Them Cabbage Down," then very simple rolls. In the space of an hour, I can get anyone to play a Scruggs-sounding thing. At least, that's what I've been doing.

GS: What kinds of changes do you see coming down the road for banjo?

TT: No seismic changes. The major thing I see now are great younger players, Noam and Greg Lift, for example—new ideas, new wrinkles on the old sounds—they're doing a lot more single-string, melody-oriented things. Very cool sound. But that's not a radical shift. Bobby Thompson and Caroll Best were doing that in the '50s—you can hear it on a Decca record, Bill Monroe on the Grand Old Opry in the '50s. With Earl Scruggs you heard more complex chord progressions, different kinds of melodies put in different contexts. And now Bela Fleck is coming out of what I was doing, plus adding jazz elements.

GS: What do you think the real value is for participants in a camp? The people who are teaching at banjo camps haven't learned at banjo camps. What's the real purpose of a banjo camp?

TT: I think some people get the big ah-ha! The light bulb goes off. I talk to people about it and, there's always inspirational value, hanging out with other banjo players. I think people learn more from participants, informally. How do you do this, and can you show me that? I know sometimes when I throw something out, it clicks for someone, and I hear, "I never got that before." It may not be a major shift, but sometimes it can be a tiny thing that makes a big difference.

Tony's Tips

One of the "tiny things" thrown out by Tony back in banjo camp was the *slide-choke*, bending a note by pushing up on the string as you slide. It makes a big difference. Here's a taste of that class so you can get the feel of what it was like. You don't have the sound track, so you can't hear Tony constantly illustrating his points on his banjo, but if you do have *Double Banjo Bluegrass Spectacular*, track two, "Bon Aqua Blues," has the lick Tony's talking about. And if you don't, just pick up your banjo and play along. You'll get the idea.

✺ ON GETTING STARTED

"Even if you're not at the stage of playing rolls, figure out the melody. Find out where the notes are. Anybody here not do that yet? Start searching; peck away. It's a really good thing, good ear training, finding simple melodies, and then filling them out with rolls."

✺ PLAYING THE SYLLABLES

"How many of you play the syllables when you play? How many of you know what that means? I heard John Hartford talking about it the first time, and he said, 'When Earl plays, he plays the syllables.' I was teaching a class like this, and he was sitting in and he said that Earl would take a song like "Ring of Fire," and he recorded it on one of his albums and took three first breaks—banjo, fiddle, mandolin, whatever it was—and each verse was different because he was playing the words for each one. And I listened to it when I got a home and, wow, he did.

"And you all know the story when he was a little kid hot-dogging it, not really playing the melody, his mom came by and said, 'Earl, I can't hear the melody, and I hear you every day, and if I can't hear it how will anybody else?'

"John Hartford would move his lips when he was playing the banjo, not when he was singing (although of course he was moving his lips then too). He would move his lips when he was taking a banjo break, and I thought it was a cute affectation because he had that cute bowler hat and he'd dance, but at this workshop I was doing, he said, 'I do that so I can match the phrasing and actually move my lips to transmit to my fingers.'"

✺ ROLLING ON THREE STRINGS

"And this is a pretty big deal; Earl does this on various tunes (*Tony plays*) like "Bugle Call Rag." This is the core position that made me play the banjo. I heard that sound, The Kingston Trio actually, and was gone. Sixteen notes ruined my life.

"Do you know the position? C7th. If you bar the 5th and pinky on the 8th fret, 1st string gives you the C7. Thing is, Earl hardly ever bars anything, so what he does up the neck is play mostly on the 1st, 2nd, and 5th strings. (*Tony plays "Shucking the Corn."*) He had to play that much into the break before he hits the 3rd string. Because the 1st, 2nd, and 5th strings are under a lot of tension, more so than the 3rd and 4th, everything snaps and crackles more up the neck (*Tony plays*) when you're just playing on the 1st, 2nd, and 5th strings.

This lick is no exception, and Earl does this lick that is all backward rolls (*he plays*), and all forward rolls (*plays*). My favorite is backward, backward, forward, backward, backward…bam, bam, bam, like drilling or something, a very hip syncopated deal. And he has a whole stash of licks that do that turn on a dime, backward and forward. Try it. It really will ennoble your play. If you get nothing else out of this entire weekend…How many of you think it's a cool lick? It is a cool lick.

OK. Leave. Go away. Thank you. Much more to talk about. Thanks for coming.

Bill Keith

THERE AT THE BEGINNING

Scrunch on over to make room around the campfire for Bill Keith.

   William Bradford Keith is one of the pioneers—and certainly the most well-known performer—of the melodic style of banjo picking that lets banjo pickers match fiddle tunes note for note. A former Bill Monroe Blue Grass Boy, Bill Keith has several Rounder records, performs internationally, and is a tireless teacher, working in banjo camps and leading banjo workshops. Bill may be most famous for producing the tabs and collaborating on the classic Earl Scruggs banjo instruction book. Along the way he invented the Keith tuners, used to alter string pitch on banjos.

GS: Hey, Bill, good to see you again. How about telling us how a Boston boy got mixed up with banjo and bluegrass.

BK: Hello. Let's see. I was born in Boston and grew up in Brockton, Massachusetts. I heard strange music late at night on WWVA in Wheeling, West Virginia. What I heard was a Bill Monroe recording and in it the sound of a banjo. I was taking piano lessons, but when I heard the banjo I told my parents I wanted to switch. We went to the local music store and they had a banjo. I didn't know anything. It was a tenor banjo, so I started by renting it, learning to play. I had a guitar teacher teaching me Dixieland music.

GS: And you were hooked?

BK: Almost. In the summer of 1957, I saw a kid playing a five-string banjo and recognized that as the sound I heard. That fall I entered Amherst College as a freshman. Within the first week, I saw a five-string

banjo for sale for $15—a cheap open back. I got Pete Seeger's book, the yellow-covered, mimeographed edition. There wasn't much in it about bluegrass three-finger style—just one transcription with the thumb always playing fifth string. That's how I started to learn. Pete Seeger's book recommended getting a record by Earl Scruggs. I did that and realized I really liked it, though it wasn't easy to learn. I set out to transcribe it and, thanks to my piano training and a pretty good ear, I just wrote down the notes I played.

GS: And that's how you built up your skills?

BK: It took me until 1958, continuing the transcriptions intensively, until my playing got pretty good. As Earl Scruggs' albums became available, I ordered them—*Flint Hill Special* and *Foggy Mountain Jamboree* were the first. After I completed military service, I moved into an apartment in Cambridge and started going to the folk music clubs like Club 47.

GS: How did you make the jump from Club 47 to the Grand Old Opry?

BK: I thought I was getting good enough to pull my weight in a band, and moved to the DC/Baltimore area. I heard there were bluegrass centers where I might get some work. In December 1962 there was a concert at Johns Hopkins with Merle Travis and Flatt and Scruggs, and the promoter was Manny Greenhill, a guy who promoted Jim Rooney and myself back in Boston. He got me into the green room after the show, and I showed my book to Earl.

GS: I imagine you were nervous. How did that first meeting go?

BK: Earl couldn't read music and couldn't read tablature, so he tested me and asked me to play it. He asked me to do "Sally Goodin" and "Home Sweet Home," and I had worked so long on those tunes I had memorized them. I didn't have to look at the music, and glanced over at Earl. His head was turned toward the music but his eyes toward my right hand. He corrected me on a couple of little things and told me he wanted me to come to Nashville to work on his book. I moved to Nashville and, while working on the book, stayed at his house as a guest.

GS: That was after Earl Scruggs and Lester Flatt left Bill Monroe and the Blue Grass Boys to go out on their own. How did you ever connect with Bill Monroe?

BK: Bill Monroe was in Nashville in the first week or so of 1963. I was staying at Earl's and would work on the book and go with him on gigs. One of the things he did was play on the Grand Old Opry, and one night I drove down with him with my banjo and played in the back rooms. Kenny Baker came in and heard me play and brought in Bill Monroe and both listened for a while. When I was leaving that evening, Kenny said Bill wanted me to come up and join the band.

GS: So you did, and I understand that meant changing your name as well?

BK: Yeah, that's pretty funny. So there wouldn't be a confusing two Bills in the band, Bill Monroe nicknamed me "Brad." A few weeks later, I recorded "Devil's Dream" and "Salt Creek" with the band.

GS: Looks like someone is trying to get your attention. See you around Woodstock.

BK: Yeah, see you all. Bye.

Janet Davis
IN LOVE WITH THE BANJO

Let me invite Janet Davis over to the campfire for just a minute. She's a real banjo legend in my book, although much too young to hit the history books.

At the very beginning of my bluegrass banjo education, I found myself stuck. I had learned a couple of songs and could read tab, but had not yet found a teacher or some reasonable direction. And then I found *Mel Bay's Back-Up Banjo* by Janet Davis. In clear, unequivocal terms, Janet Davis laid out a complete bluegrass banjo system with tab and musical notation, identifying roll patterns, chord progressions, passing tones, etc.

I attacked "John Hardy" like I was the sheriff on his trail, relentlessly playing simple lead and backup variations, with Janet's no-nonsense voice and crisp banjo supporting me on my studio boom box. She taught at both Smoky Mountain Banjo Academy and Banjo Camp North, and she wasn't the least fearsome in person. Quiet, with a soft Texas drawl and an easy way about her, Janet Davis loves banjo. Classically trained as a pianist and a graduate in music from the University of Texas (Austin), she's a major participant in banjo camps, as you'll see.

GS: Come on over to the fire, Janet. Welcome.

JD: Hi, everybody. Nice to be here.

GS: You came to the banjo after college, playing mostly blues guitar at folk clubs around the Austin area in the Kingston Trio era is that right?

JD: That's right.

GS: But at some point you elected to focus on teaching.

JD: I wanted to share it. Banjo is such a wonderful instrument. I wanted to give it the respect it deserved. I taught a lot of professional people, and medical doctors particularly seemed to take to it. I knew how it works, I knew how to teach it, and I wanted to share it. I love the banjo.

GS: You seem to have done that through your popular Mel Bay and Hal Leonard banjo books and DVDs, yet you still teach at several banjo camps.

JD: Banjo camps are great. The impact, the spirit is just wonderful, everybody has the same interest. It's all about this one instrument. What's so interesting to me is when they start, no one knows anyone and everyone is a little formal. It's so much fun to see everyone this afternoon, starting to pick together, talk to each other, because they begin to know each other from the classes. The classes are small and informal enough that everyone can participate.

GS: What isn't small and intimate is the major music store operation you started. Janet Davis Music, offering everything from instruments and strings to CDs and books, is a powerful presence in the banjo world, with more than 50,000 active customers worldwide. But even there, you're involved in banjo camps.

JD: That's true. To help support banjo camps, and make it possible for kids to attend, we donate instruments, recorders, and other gear to be raffled off for scholarship funds at a few of the larger programs.

GS: You had a big influence on me, Janet. I've always wanted to ask you how you feel about practicing banjo.

JD: I have a theory about that word. I play all the time. And I make use of my playing time by working on things, but it's fun. And when I teach I don't like to call it practice, especially to kids. I say, "Play every single day." And I don't have time right now, because of this business, to sit down and do it, but I could play four to 17 hours a day, like a professional musician, for myself, because I love it that much. But I don't consider myself a performer.

GS: Well, you are certainly modest. So let me brag about you to the folks around the campfire. I was at a workshop where Janet played with Eric ("Dueling Banjos") Weissberg, swapping lead and backup, and if you turned your head away, you couldn't tell who was playing what part.

JD: I don't know about that, but thank you. And on that note, I'll be saying goodnight to everyone.

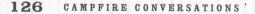

Brad Leftwich
A DIFFERENT AESTHETIC

One of the top-ranked old-time banjo players is someone you don't know. And it's unlikely you know the name of a fiddle player who is so highly regarded that he played at the White House and is a major influence in old-time music.

It's easy to remember the names of these players since they're both the same guy—Brad Leftwich.

"Top" and "highest" aren't words you find readily in the old-time music lexicon. This most laid-back and cooperative of musical backwaters generally shuns competitive awards. But Leftwich, by any measure, is certainly one of the most highly regarded old-time fiddlers and banjo players in the world. Despite this double achievement, his is not a household name, not even in the southern heartland. It's only within the dedicated, hard-core old-time music subculture that Brad is universally recognized.

Gail Gillespie, editor of *Old Time Herald*, the industry trade paper and community newsletter for old-time, explains his exalted status among old-time musicians: "Brad is just a great, charismatic musician. His playing is clean, brilliant. He is a musician's musician, embedded in the tradition, inspired by the best of traditional music."

In this rarefied world, Brad Leftwich has a unique position. Most of the roots musicians on whose work old-time music is based have passed on. Until recently, contemporary artists like Bob Carlin, David Holt, and John Herrmann headed for Galax, Virginia, or the Round Peak area in Surry County, North Carolina, to listen and learn from Fred Cockerham, Tommy Jarrell, and others, or they headed deep into the hollers and hills of Appalachia to find other original sources. With few exceptions, that era is over. The appearance of

88-year-old fiddler Joe Thompson with the Carolina Chocolate Drops at the Swannanoa Gathering in 2007 may have been the only time many in the audience had heard the authentic sound of old-time music live.

For Brad Leftwich, however, old-time music is very much alive. It's his native culture. His father sang old-time country songs and backed them on guitar. His grandfather, a cousin of Tommy Jarrell's wife, played the five-string banjo. His grandfather, from Carroll County, Virginia, near the Round Peak area, moved from Virginia to Kansas in 1907. Brad grew up in Oklahoma.

He started playing banjo when he was 15 and the fiddle a couple of years later, spending time at Virginia and North Carolina fiddlers' conventions and learning from musicians he met there. It wasn't too many years later before Brad won the Super Bowl of old-time—the famed Clifftop (West Virginia) Old-Time Music Festival fiddle contest. In that same year, 1990, his old-time band, The Humdingers, won the band contest as well.

His teaching of old-time banjo has been somewhat limited to workshops and banjo camps, but Brad does have a highly regarded Mel Bay book, *Round Peak Style Clawhammer Banjo*, that comes with a CD. Move in close as Brad joins the campfire circle…he talks quietly.

GS: Welcome, Brad. Can we get right to the exclusive nature of old-time music? There are people who say old-time music consists of songs from a culture that no longer exists, played to an elite audience.

BL: It's true that this music came out of the rural South in the 19th century, and that culture is essentially gone, but the music has made the transition. People are playing and creating this music, turning out to hear it and learn it. The music we like and play and recognize is a pre-commercial kind of music that came out of a tradition. People playing now are making a choice to play that music. It may be a little more self-conscious choice than it was in the past, but it's not a museum piece. People like this music; they like to get together, play it, and dance. There are a lot of communities around the country where this music is popular.

GS: What do you think of the idea that most of this music comes from fiddle tunes that, to mainstream ears, sound astonishingly…well, bad.

BL: So much of being an old-time musician is learning to listen through superficial stuff. The music is very deep. That's why a lot of people don't get it. I've heard people say things like, "This stuff is awful. It's out of tune, scratchy, this guy can barely play." For somebody like me listening to somebody like Joe Thompson, that just doesn't matter. It's totally superficial. You have to hear the music underneath that.

People just don't know how to listen; they're expecting the music to be something other than what it is. If you go to India, for example, and you can't understand the music, or when unenlightened people say Chinese music sounds like pots and pans falling down the stairs, they just don't know what they're listening to.

GS: What about the quality of original recorded material? Doesn't that make this music less accessible?

BL: The problem with listening to an old-time fiddler like Ed Haley is that lots of recordings are totally worn out. Some field recordings were of inferior quality

in the first place. Old-time musicians get really used to ignoring the superficial stuff and listening to the music underneath. Haley was a remarkable musician, technically near the top of the range. His was a really complicated style of playing, very elaborate, one of the best. The real issue, however, is not the quality of recorded material.

Tommy Jarrell is a really good example. I've heard people criticize Tommy's intonation and tone production. They're listening but totally missing the point—they're not hearing. They assume he would sound like a violinist if only he knew how, but in fact Tommy is playing exactly the way he wants to play. He didn't care for violin music at all.

Most people listen to mainstream fiddle music and are used to a violin sounding clear, as in classical music. You have to learn how to listen to Tommy's music, understand the structure and technique he uses. I'm not saying that Tommy was playing out of tune. He's playing exactly what he wants to play, but it's a different aesthetic. He's not using a tempered scale; he's playing a lot of blue notes, much like old black music scales and neutral tones, not like a scale a classically trained musician might use. The dissonance, the rasps and scrapes of the bow, are all an intentional part of the music, and to most old-time musicians, the music would sound bland and gutless without it.

GS: I've seen lots of old-time banjo players like you gravitate toward the fiddle. Is that because there are inherent limitations to the banjo?

BL: Limitations to the banjo? Do you mean within the instrument? It sort of depends. If you want to play something besides traditional music on it, maybe. To play within a traditional style, I don't feel limited. I can sit down and play traditional tunes in traditional style. There are people who want to turn it into a solo concert instrument, do all sorts of fancy stuff not conceived of in a traditional context. They do feel limited and try to figure ways around those limitations, and I respect that. But what I want to do on the banjo is play traditional tunes the way they have been played for generations.

GS: Your Round Peak clawhammer book presents some of those traditional tunes in tab. What's your feeling about that?

BL: *Round Peak Style Clawhammer Banjo* is not really an instructional book, but more about the repertoire. I had ambivalent feelings about the tab. I like the book. I think the CD in the back is more important than the tab. My recommendation to people is to listen to the CD until the music is stuck in their heads. If they have trouble getting a certain sound, then they can refer to the tablature to see exactly what notes are being played and how they're being played.

I don't like to teach with tablature because the minute I give somebody a piece of tablature, they stop paying attention to me. It's so important in this kind of music to be able to listen and to imitate, so it's crucial

to be focused on the musician and the music instead of a piece of paper with markings on it. There's tension at a banjo camp. There's a certain subset of students really dependent on that piece of paper. They really want it. What I do is teach the tune aurally, force them to use their ear and listening skills, and a day or two later give them the tablature.

GS: Speaking of tabs, what's that you're holding?

BL: It's the tab for one of my favorite songs, "Callaway." I handed it out at the end of my workshop today. Thought you might like a copy.

GS: Thanks, Brad. And thanks for joining us. Sounds like a jam is starting up around the fire.

BL: Good night. See you in the morning.

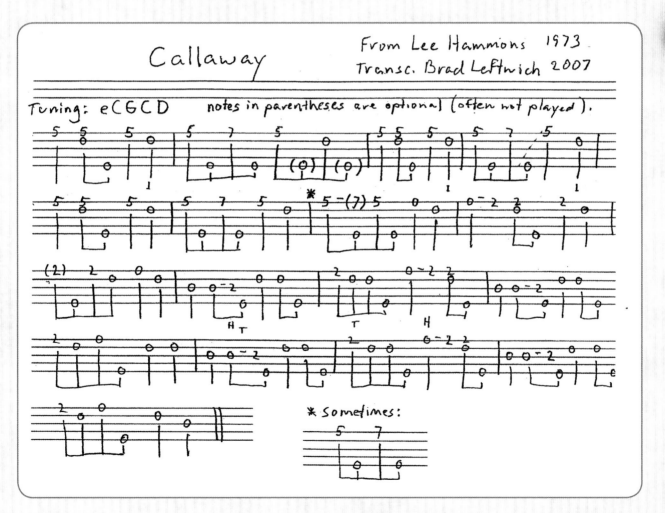

John Herrmann
VIEWS OF AN EX-BUSKER

John Herrmann is the quintessential old-time musician. Best known for his banjo and fiddle playing, he's been playing and teaching old-time music for nearly 40 years all over the world. John has been a busker in the great tradition of gypsies, minstrels, and jongleurs, who earn their money entertaining in the streets and at festivals. From 1977 to 1982, John played in the parks and boulevards of Europe and Asia. His far-ranging ideas on old-time music, banjos, and culture are worth hearing around the campfire before we head back for a late-night jam session.

GS: Good evening, John.

JH: Hello.

GS: To get things going, would you mind repeating your line about old-time music?

JH: Sure. A bluegrass fiddler said to me, "Old-time music is kind of like a joke I don't get."

GS: John, I must admit that the first time I saw you perform, you walked onstage, didn't smile, sat down, and played, and left. I didn't get it. A couple of weeks ago I heard you play. You were playing banjo on the streets of Asheville with an old-time string quartet. An excited crowd surrounded you all, and there was a hatful of money at your feet.

JH: A hatful? Really?

GS: Yes, and way more amazing was the way you were pounding on your banjo, belting out song after song. You didn't seem like the same guy I met at Banjo Camp North! And this time there was no question about

getting it. Everybody got it—foot stomping, hand-clapping, dancing-in-the-streets getting it! Who were those guys?

JH: The fiddler was John Engle, and Amy Hobbs was on bass. Tom Klintworth played guitar. At that time we called ourselves The Toejammers, but lately we've been using The Wiretappers.

GS: You've been part of several significant old-time groups. But these days how much busking are you still doing?

JH: Not much. Mostly I teach at camps and play music, but I travel more for gigs. I don't do workshops and private teaching, and I don't do any promotion. I'm not interested in self-promotion. I find it really distasteful, even though I understand why people do it.

GS: I read you're a lifelong Zen practitioner, and you have an MA from Johns Hopkins in creative writing.

JH: True.

GS: And you're a hell of a musician. Besides banjo, you play fiddle, guitar, harmonica, mandolin, ukulele, and bass. How come you play so many instruments?

JH: I basically play old-time music, and in old-time each instrument is a tool for doing a very limited thing. I learned to play old-time music on all those instruments, which is not the same as mastering all those instruments. I learned how to play them because I'd be hanging out with friends and there would be a session, and I would never want to be the second banjo or third fiddle, so I learned how to play lots of instruments so I could always sit in.

GS: Is there anything you find limiting about old-time banjo?

JH: Yes, it's limited by its essential rhythmic function. You could extend that with music technique, but then it would no longer be old-time banjo. One of the differences between old-time and bluegrass is that old-time banjo has a certain function that is circumscribed, whereas bluegrass has taken on a jazz aesthetic, and you can do whatever you want technically.

GS: Do you have a working definition of old-time?

JH: Yes, it's the traditional music that people played for themselves when their culture was intact, before it got wiped out by America and the media. Think about what happened to old-time Appalachian music and culture. There was old-time music across the country. It only lasted longer in the mountains.

GS: Why is this music so special to you?

JH: Old-time is like lots of music that I love—it's not necessarily pretty. Like raku pottery or driftwood, it's rough. It has a beauty that's not pretty.

GS: But in fact, there is a strong sentiment within the old-time music community about what music actually qualifies.

JH: There are two things going on there: One is music and the other is anthropology. All the things about preserving old-time music as it is and the culture, that's anthropology. Anthropologists are more interested in an old guy from the culture who is a terrible fiddler than a young, hot fiddler who's not from the culture. Anthropologists are more interested in a shard of pottery from 30,000 BC than a beautiful pot made yesterday. They're not interested in the art—they're interested in the anthropological value, and that's a different thing.

I have a little bit of anthropological interest in old-time music because it preserves Appalachian culture, but I am more interested in music that is this thing that people do together that takes them to a certain place. And that can be done with lots of different kinds of music. I'm interested in old-time music specifically because I think its simplicity and directness is a really good vehicle for going to a musical place. I also think that there are a lot of us who are interested in old-time music because we don't have a vital culture of our own to tap into. We have this kind of hodgepodge culture. And I think it's true of most people living in the Appalachians now. They're not connected to Appalachian culture, hardly at all.

I think a lot of people can learn this music and go to that deep musical place. It doesn't take the development that jazz takes. And the instruments aren't expensive.

GS: That may be true but I've seen several open-back banjos that cost over $5,000.

JH: I would be perfectly happy with your banjo…

GS: This crappy aluminum pot banjo?

JH: …if that's all I had to play. I could live with that. People who spend a lot on banjos are interested in something more than just a good banjo.

GS: What about yours?

JH: It's an old Dobsonesque banjo, probably made around 1880. It doesn't have any name on it. I found it in an electric guitar store in Charlottesville and paid $75 for it.

GS: Any modifications on your banjo?

JH: Nothing special. I do some things, loosen the head so it's not too bright, and stuff a rag in the back to take out the overtones—not to quiet it down, but to make it plunky. I use light strings, but I play banjos with medium strings and get along with them. I figure I could take any banjo and make it playable. One thing different: I sometimes put duct tape over the bridge to make it sound like gut. If someone gave me an old Mastertone, which is way too bright, I might put duct tape on the strings.

GS: Going from the global to the very local, would you mind telling me which finger you use to pick your banjo?

JH: I use the middle finger on the first string and the index finger on all the others. I thought I was the only one to do it, but I found out there are a lot of old-time players who do that. It used to be all the melodic clawhammer players would use the middle finger and all the rocking southern-style players used the index. And

I just started using both because I found it was more economical for me, and then I found out a lot of people are doing it. When I do that cluck sound, if I'm leading with my index finger on the first string, I have to come back, but if I'm leading with my middle finger, the index can just follow it through for the harmonic cluck sound.

GS: Thanks so much for sharing this information with us tonight, John.

JH: Good night, all.

Wayne Erbsen
THE WHOLE THOUSAND NOTES

Another Southern Californian who came to the Appalachia region and fell in love with the music, the people, and the area, and stayed to make his mark, Wayne divides his time somewhat unevenly. He's a performer, teacher, writer, and publisher, sometimes all at once.

Wayne Erbsen's cabin in the East Asheville hills is part of a wooded enclave that houses, not only his home and music studio, but a thriving publishing industry, under the banner Native Ground Books & Music. Two of the books, unless you live in a banjo-less universe, you have likely seen: *Bluegrass Banjo for the Complete Ignoramus*, and the similarly named clawhammer version. He's written and published 23 others—Civil War ballads, country humor, log cabin songs and stories, Southern mountain classics, well, you get the idea. An adjunct instructor in Appalachian Music at Warren Wilson College, Erbsen has a serious academic side, but is probably best known as an

author/publisher, except to his local contingent of students, who flock to his log cabin for lessons and jam sessions. He has a distinct teaching approach that shows up in his workshops, private lessons, and books. Let's bring Wayne Erbsen into the campfire circle.

GS: Welcome to Blue Mountain Banjo Camp, Wayne.

WE: Nice to be here.

GS: Tell me about your approach to teaching the banjo.

WE: I believe most instruction books and instructors start their students off way too hard. My approach is to introduce the bare skeleton, the tune and a verse, and add a lick and a couple of chords. If you go out and buy a Christmas tree, you don't buy it with all the bells and whistles on it. You buy it bare, and then you add your own ornaments onto it, varying year to year.

Every manual I've seen teaches the whole thousand notes that are "Cripple Creek"—and that's "Cripple Creek." And it's like a straitjacket 'cause you have to play it just that way. It's too many notes and it's too complicated. It doesn't lend itself to improvisation or individual creative choice. Learn it that way, and you're stuck with an arrangement.

GS: Is it fair to say that you're a product of banjo camps? You attended Idylwyld Camp as a kid, meeting Jean Ritchie and Jimmy Driftwood, picking up bluegrass rolls from Claude Reeves.

WE: That's right. Reeves suggested that I pick up a Flat and Scruggs album. And that was the real beginning of my bluegrass banjo education.

GS: But you're not exclusively a banjo picker…

WE: True. I also play other string instruments—fiddle, mandolin, and guitar. Most bluegrass pickers can play guitar, some, but that's it. I like them all, and I teach camp workshops in all those instruments, plus string band and voice.

GS: What's your favorite teaching experience?

WE: That would have to be back around 1984, with Bob Willoughby and Fred Park. We started the Swannanoa School of Southern Music and Dance on the Warren Wilson campus, a resident program that led directly to the Swannanoa Gathering.

GS: That was a great idea. Coming from the high-intensity bluegrass programs of SMBA and Banjo Camp North, thinking how hard you guys worked to refine your technique and get on top of your instrument technically, I gotta ask: How good are you at bluegrass?

WE: I'm pretty good at the Ralph Stanley kind of bluegrass. I'm more a song-and-tune kind of player.

GS: For anyone straddling old-time and bluegrass, I'd say that's a perfect answer. Finally, what kind of banjo do you play?

WE: This right here is a Montgomery Ward.

Pete Seeger
REFLECTIONS

Pete Seeger participated in the Tennessee Banjo Institute, the very first banjo camp. Forty years earlier, in 1949, he created the first banjo camp in a book. His *How to Play the Five-String Banjo*, complete with pictures, songs, and lessons, has been the entry point for banjo players for more than a half century.

That little book, however, is almost the least of what he has accomplished. He has performed both for presidents and armies of impoverished marchers. He has protested on the side of the road and sailed the Hudson River, campaigning for clean water.

Through this all he has been a defender of traditional music, as well as a beloved singer and banjo player. His handmade, long-necked banjo has been both a trusted instrument for universal justice and freedom, and a source of great pleasure for music lovers. Recipient of the Presidential Medal of the Arts and granted the Library of Congress Living Legend designation, Pete Seeger is more than a national treasure. With his lifelong commitment to justice for the world, he has been a beacon of sanity.

A young Pete Seeger and the Weavers helped launch the folk revolution of the '40s and '50s. His protest songs, such as "Where Have All the Flowers Gone?" and "If I Had a Hammer," covered by singers everywhere, have passed into American traditional music. A passionate environmentalist and defender of civil rights, Seeger, who was brought before the infamous McCarthy committee, defended himself not by "taking the Fifth" but by claiming our Constitutional First Amendment right of association. For that, he was blackballed, indicted, and imprisoned. Let's find out what he's up to these days.

GS: Good evening, Pete.

PS: Hello, there.

GS: What are you currently working on?

PS: I'm putting the final touches on the revision of my sing-along memoir, *Where Have All the Flowers Gone?* I'm still working on a few pages, getting out little mistakes I thought I got out four years ago. It'll be published in the fall of 2008 by the folk magazine *Sing Out!* I'm a firm believer in amending things, trying to improve them. I wouldn't still be married after 64 years if I hadn't learned a lot of things from my wife—like how to wash dishes and sweep floors, among other things.

GS: Can we talk about some of your banjo ideas? Where do you see banjo music going?

PS: The banjo has a unique tone, needle points of sound, a little bit like a harpsichord. Earl Scruggs took it and showed that extraordinary things could be done with it. What he did was take African syncopation, dividing eight notes into 3-3-2—common enough in West Africa and Latin America—but Scruggs did it lightning fast. And now people like Bela Fleck and Tony Trischka have carried it far beyond.

But we're just at the beginning, I'd say, of learning the subtleties of rhythm that Africa and Asia, too, have to offer. Europe had extraordinary melody and harmony, but when it came to rhythm, even our greats like Beethoven were really writing kindergarten music— "German stamping music," a friend calls it.

India and China, Japan too, have similar instruments, but they haven't been developed as far as the banjo. That's one of the great things America has done—develop things invented by other cultures.

Pete Seeger, performing on stage at Yorktown Heights High School, Yorktown, N.Y. / *World Journal Tribune* photo by James Kavallines.

GS: There is a strong interest in banjo on the part of retired people. How do you account for that?

PS: I think people in the second half of their lives are looking for things that can make them feel happy. It's easy to feel discouraged when you're old. I made mistakes in life; I failed here, I failed there. Banjo and its sparkling rhythm can cheer you up.

GS: Are you playing banjo much now?

PS: I pick a tune occasionally. I keep my banjo hanging on the wall, and I take it down and play. I also play a 12-string guitar, more than my six-string guitar.

GS: What banjo do you play?

PS: This is the same one I put together 50 years ago. It has a Vega head, and I built the neck out of the world's hardest wood—*lignum vitae*. They use it for marine bearings. I bought a piece of the wood and had someone with a power saw shape it, and I rounded it off with a file and sanded it. Then I had someone put in the frets.

One banjo got swiped; another got broken on a freight train. No one played banjo in the 1930s when I started. I bought the second banjo, a Vega Whyte

Laydie, for $10 at a hockshop. That one got stolen. I left it in the car, went in for a cup of coffee, and when I came out it was gone. I had a couple of others, but I wasn't satisfied with them, so I ended up buying a Vega head and making my own long neck.

GS: Pretty much everybody credits your *How to Play the Five-String Banjo* as their introduction to the banjo. How did it come about?

PS: I'm quite proud of that little banjo book I improvised in 1948. My father (Charles Seeger) said, "Did you ever think of writing up a manual for the banjo? The old ones are too formal. You could make one much more informal." So I sat down at the typewriter, wrote it, and then mimeographed 100 copies. It took four years to sell those hundred copies.

GS: And I understand that in one of the earliest examples of open-handed, open-source creativity, you published the "red cover" revised second edition in 1954 without copyright. In your prefatory remarks you wrote, "The first edition said 'Copyright 1948.' This we fear was a falsehood. The necessary four bucks were never shelled out. Permission is hereby given to reprint whenever needed."

PS: Yes, that's true.

GS: You mentioned your father. Was he an important musical influence on you?

PS: My father was one of the founders of ethno-musicology. Early on he was the youngest full professor at Berkeley (the University of California), in charge of building the music department. He was fired for making speeches against imperialist war, and then got the grand idea of building one of the first automobile trailers, using hand tools. They didn't have plywood in those days, and he put it together using maple wood and brass screws, hard rubber wheels, and a canvas top like a covered wagon. He said we could take our beautiful music out to the towns and countryside like the Chautauqua tour. It was a complete failure. The Model T Ford was lucky to make 25 miles an hour over

Prof. Chas. Louis Seeger & family, May 23, 1921
Library of Congress Prints and Photographs Division. National Photo Company Collection

the bumpy dirt roads, and we almost got drowned in a small flood. My mother had to wash my diapers in a pot over an open fire, and once I fell into the fire, and if I hadn't been yanked out a few seconds later, I would have been killed. My mother put her foot down, and they went back to New York. They were teachers at Julliard when I was a child.

GS: That's quite a story. Considering how passionate you have been about social and environmental causes, I wonder what kind of role you see music and the five-string banjo playing in the future.

PS: I am convinced that banjo picking is one of the things that will save the world because music is one of the things that will save the world. If there is a human race here in a hundred years, banjo is going to be one of the main reasons.

GS: On that note…

PS: Keep on, everyone.

Homework

Practice Tips from the Experts

Most everybody agrees that practicing banjo is the key to your development as a musician, but the nature of practice varies wildly. There are those who follow rigorous warm-up routines and build their practice sessions around scales, chord changes, and exercises. Others focus on learning new songs or working on technique. In developing your own practice routines, you don't have to go it alone. There's lots of available advice from excellent teachers and performers out there. Because they don't all agree, you get to pick and choose your own form of practice.

In the workshops and campfire conversations at Blue Mountain Banjo Camp, you've already come across some excellent ideas. Here are a few more thoughts worth considering.

❁ PETE WERNICK'S IDEAS TO HONE YOUR SKILLS

+ Listen to recordings of yourself. You'll hear things you don't notice when you're busy playing.
+ Focus your practicing around developing your sense of:

Melody—On the neck of the banjo, work out each melody note of a song you can hum. Do a new song every week.

Pulse—Practice with a metronome, or better yet, a rhythm machine. Learn to emphasize every note that occurs on a beat (first and fifth notes of the roll).

Meaning—Cultivate your ability to play differently, depending on the mood of the song, and the actions and images in the lyrics. Use dynamics and accenting, using the whole neck.

Clarity of sound and of purpose—Be aware of the effects you're trying to achieve, and ask yourself if the listener is really hearing good and interesting banjo sounds.

❊ BRAD LEFTWICH ON HIS OWN PRACTICE

I don't really practice a lot. When I was learning to play I still didn't practice. At least not in the sense that I'd call it "practice"—when you're sitting there working out one riff over and over again. I played tunes. I still play a lot. I think this is important, although it may not work for everybody. In the course of teaching, if I see somebody having trouble with technique, I'd help figure out what the problems were and how to work around them. Every case would be a little different. In general, I think most people have to work on timing, especially in banjo playing. Make sure it's even and the timing is impeccable. A lot of people don't understand how critical that is.

❊ STEVE KAUFMAN'S STYLE

I tell everyone to take the time they have allocated and divide it in half: the first half is for work on old stuff. Don't warm up; just start off slow. Make a song list, and in the first half of your practice period, however long it is, work on old stuff.

First half

Get a loose-leaf notebook and leave the first five pages open for song titles. Write them down in columns—handwrite them, don't put it in Word or alphabetize them. You're going to learn lots of simple songs. And don't spend a lot of time working on a huge piece. It's just a waste of time you could be spending learning tunes.

Flip over five pages and write a song title, say, "Boil Them Cabbage Down," page one. Now start your repetitions. You've got your technique to work on in the first hour as you slowly, correctly, play the tune without making mistakes. Learn the spaces, not the notes. That's the timing. You have to get rock-solid timing; the content isn't as important as the timing.

Next, you play a song five times and put down five tick marks on the page—another five times, another five ticks—until you fill the whole page with tick marks; and when you do—when the page is black with tick marks—you're all through with that song. You'll never have to learn it again. You have it for the rest of your life.

You leave five pages blank for titles so you can learn 2,000 songs.

Second half

And that's the first half of your practice. The second half is to try new stuff like sight reading or transposing songs, or learning one new chord and finding a way to place it, or a new chord position. Each individual can come up with stuff that's new and important.

Schedule out your time this way and you'll always move forward. Use a timer. When the timer goes DING you start on the new stuff, more than likely in the middle of something. When it goes DING again, you move on.

And I definitely recommend a metronome. The metronome is your friend. And use a recorder so you can hear yourself and see where you need to do work. You do this schedule Monday through Friday. No practicing over the weekend, but you can play. You can't be constantly practicing or you'll get burned out.

I don't do scales. Scales tell you what notes can be played in a key. You have to know all the scales, but you can learn 30 fiddle tunes in the key of D and know all those notes.

JAMES MCKINNEY'S APPROACH

Practice. You have to think about it as a battle. No, it's a war. You have to have a practice goal written down on a piece of paper. It can be as simple as, OK, I know I have an hour. First five minutes I'm going to visualize my fingerboard. Then the next, my finger exercises. Then work on those scales. I make a concise list of what I'm going to do. Once I make that list, I get my watch out and hang it on my music stand. My most important tools are my tape recorder and my metronome.

I'm a big proponent of listening to the right thing. You've got to be selective. You have to know the song, and if called on you have to play it just like Earl. You're improving around the changes, but you're not playing it if you can't play it like he did. You can get it close enough to sound like him. So it's important to educate yourself about the original guy who wrote it, because that's theme. Everything else is variations on that theme.

Thinking about tone

The other thing you have to do is think about tone. Practicing is not just the notes. You have to play with tone and timing and a sense of touch. You cannot over-learn a tune. You cannot practice it too much. If you haven't played "Foggy Mountain Breakdown" 5,000 times, you're not even scratching the surface. A lot of people move on. We're all anxious to learn as much as we can, but if we learn 30 tunes and they're barely recognizable, what good is that? It's better to get one down.

Play real slow. The way to smooth out a piece is to go SLOW, and make sure all notes have the same beat. Most people will speed up on the easy parts and slow down on the hard parts. The right way is to keep the beat, keep it all the same.

There's a way to practice using looping when you're learning new tunes. Take four notes of tablature, max, and then turn that piece of paper over. Not just "I'm not looking at it." I mean turn it over. Then double check. Do that about five times and then take a mental break, and then do it again. Next, do the next four notes and turn the page back over. And now you've got all eight notes, so you need to loop those notes. I don't loop fours, but I loop eights, or the whole section. The looping will get you there quick.

J.D. ROBINSON'S PHILOSOPHY

Quit practicing; never practice again. All you gotta do is "Do It." If you do it a bunch of times, you get better at it. But the "bunch of times" may number in the thousands!

THE Todd Wright WORKSHOP

How to Set Up & Maintain Your Banjo

I met Todd Wright at Banjo Camp North, when he tuned up my Deering Sierra. He's unique in the banjo world in a few respects. For one thing, while today he's head of Artist Relations and Events at Deering Banjo Company, where he supports producers and artists at major festivals, banjo camps, and concerts, in the past he had a similar role at Gibson Banjos.

There just aren't that many guys who have top-level banjo setup experience with both of America's biggest banjo makers, while also working with the leading banjo pickers. Actually, there is only one. So Todd was our first call for this final workshop at Blue Mountain Banjo Camp, the focus being the care and feeding of the star of this camp—the banjo itself.

Beyond his technical talents, Todd is an accomplished musician, comfortable on most stringed instruments, as well as an experienced teacher.

Todd did his apprenticeship as a luthier with Fred Artindale in San Luis Obispo, California, and continued on this path, building and repairing stringed instruments with Glen Woodruff in the San Francisco Bay Area before moving to the South to be in the middle of the booming old-time and bluegrass music scene. He played old-time music in North Carolina, around Raleigh and Chapel Hill, before settling right over the Smoky Mountains in the rural community of Grassy Fork, Tennessee. It was there that he and his partners, Zeke McDonald and Jesper Peterson, formed The Smoky Mountain Instrument Works, to manufacture and sell Appalachian string instruments.

It was during this time that Todd met his musical mentor, old-time banjo player Ralph Ford. He performed with Ralph until Ralph's passing in 1980.

Being so close to Pigeon Forge, it was inevitable that Todd would take his banjo, fiddle, and guitar over to Dollywood where, for several years, he was a featured performer, playing old-time, bluegrass, and country music by day and performing at the Hee Haw Theater in the evenings with Archie Campbell, Red Rector, and guests like Chet Atkins and Grandpa Jones.

Todd buckled down to a different kind of life when he joined Gibson Banjo in Nashville, first as a clinician and then, later, handling artist relations and events, sales and marketing, much as he does for Deering today. In a nutshell, that's Todd Wright.

Remember how I told you at the beginning of camp how my introduction to playing the banjo was Pete Seeger's book, *How to Play the Five-String Banjo?* Turns out, that's how Todd got introduced to the banjo. So, I think that completes the circle to end this session of Blue Mountain Banjo Camp with Todd's workshop. Whether you play old-time or bluegrass, you're in good hands. Without further ado, here's your professor with his prescription for a happy banjo.

LESSON: THE HAPPY BANJO

During our time together, I will be sharing with you some concepts and techniques that will help you bring the best out of your instrument. Over the past 40 years, in my career as an instrument builder, repairman, performer, and clinician, I have had the privilege of spending time with many of the greatest players and builders in the banjo world. They have always been generous with their knowledge and expertise, and now I have the opportunity to pass their insights on to you.

One thing to keep in mind is that good banjo tone is a very subjective point. Also what sounds good to you now may not be to your liking as your ear and technique progress. There are also seasonal changes that call for minor adjustments, and it will be good for you to become experienced and comfortable at making these adjustments yourself. I'd encourage you to keep an open mind to the ideas presented, not only here, but also from other sources you find. We banjo enthusiasts can be rather opinionated—just remember the most important opinion is yours.

In the first section of this workshop, we'll focus on two areas. The first area is techniques and adjustments that affect tone and playability. The second section is dedicated to daily maintenance tips, and quarterly or seasonal maintenance suggestions.

Well, get your banjos out and let's get started!

Adjusting for Tone and Playability

✷ TONE

First, an overview of the basic tone-producing components:

- Tightness of the head
- Height and density of the bridge
- Tailpiece adjustment
- String gauge
- Adjustment of the coordinator rods

Head tension is adjusted by tightening the hex nuts on the hooks or brackets that rest on the flange or bracket shoe. This pulls the tension hoop down over the rim, tightening the head. The tighter the head, the brighter the banjo will sound; the looser the head, the more low-end you will hear. Both extremes reach points of diminishing returns. It's important for the head to be tightened evenly around the rim.

Measure the distance from the tension hoop to the tone ring or bottom of the rim and keep it uniform. About ¾ inch in from the rim, while muting the strings, tap the head near each bracket, and listen to the pitch to be sure the tension is even.

There's a lot of conflicting information about tuning the head. I don't think there is one pitch that suits all banjos. I do feel that each banjo has its own optimum resonant frequency, and with close attention and patience, you can find the tension that best complements your instrument. By listening carefully as you tighten or loosen the head, you will find a degree of tension that your banjo's resonance responds to.

The bridge is probably the easiest thing to change on the banjo and has a huge influence on the sound produced. Some general rules that apply are: The less mass in the bridge, the brighter the end product; the more mass, the bassier it will sound. For a bluegrass banjo, $\frac{5}{8}$ inch is a standard height. A taller bridge will usually produce more volume but may also require adjustments to affect the string height.

There has been much experimentation with bridge materials and shape, and I encourage you to try several bridges to find your favorite. The variety and availability of high-quality ones are outstanding these days. The density of a bridge can be determined by counting the end grain visible on the ends of the bridge. Another tip is from violinmakers. They drop the bridge on a hard surface and listen to the sound it makes. A higher-pitched sound will produce a brighter sounding banjo.

Tailpiece adjustment is another area of opposing opinions. Some like a tailpiece tightened down as close to the head as possible for a very bright sound. This may also cause the setup to feel tight. Others prefer just enough tension to keep the bridge in place, which results in a warmer sound. This is a choice

for you to make according to your personal preference. You can easily adjust the tailpiece while the strings are tuned to pitch by pressing down on it while turning the set screw on the end of the tailpiece. The base of the tailpiece should fit snuggly on the top of the tension hoop to prevent any buzzing.

String gauge affects the volume and tone of the banjo. The lighter the string, the brighter the sound; the heavier the string, the more bass and volume. Also the lighter string vibrates in a wider arc and is more prone to buzz at lower string height.

The coordinator rods should hold the neck tight to the rim by pulling on the lag bolts. This is an often-overlooked area that can have a noticeable effect on tone and volume. To check the coordinator rods, loosen the hex nuts on the rods. They usually take a $\frac{1}{2}$-inch wrench. Then insert a nail in the hole in the rod and check the tightness. It should be firm with no slack. Don't over-tighten, as the lag bolts can be stripped or broken. Then, while holding the nail to keep the rod tight, re-tighten the hex nuts.

✳ PLAYABILITY

Now here's an overview of the factors
influencing playability:

* Height of nut
* Height of bridge
* Placement of bridge
* Neck relief
* Angle of the neck
* String gauge

The nut slots should be cut to leave about $\frac{1}{16}$-inch
clearance between the bottom of the string and the top
of the first fret. Slots should be angled to match the slant
of the peghead and with a slight V to prevent buzzing or
pinching of the string. Graphite from a lead pencil placed
in the slot helps the string to move smoothly while tuning.

A higher bridge affects the tone by increasing the
amount of downward pressure exerted on the head. It affects
the playability by raising or lowering the string height.
Another factor is the string spacing on the bridge. Some
players find a slightly wider spacing allows them to attack
the strings with more power, thus producing more volume.

Placement of the bridge affects the instrument's ability
to play in tune, especially in the higher positions. The
correct placement can be located by using a ruler
to measure the distance from the nut to the 12th fret. Then
measure the same distance from the 12th fret to the bridge
top, and you have a close starting point.

Due to the string being depressed while being
fretted, some compensation is necessary. To achieve this it
is common to match the open string sound with the sound
of the string fretted at the 12th fret. An electronic tuner is
helpful with this process. Another approach is to sound the
harmonic at the 12th fret and match it to the fretted note at
the same fret. You need to go through this process on both
D strings to find the correct bridge position.

Neck relief is the term given to the practice of
putting a slight forward bow in the fingerboard. This
is to help prevent string buzz as you move up the
fingerboard. A good way to check the relief is to hold
the string down at the 1st and 22nd fret; there should
be enough clearance to pass a business card under the
string at the 9th fret.

The **angle of the neck**, in combination with the
bridge height, affects the string height as you move
up the neck. Preferences for string height at the 12th
fret range from about $\frac{1}{8}$ to $\frac{3}{4}$ inch. The neck angle is
determined by the heel cut that is precision-fit to the rim
during manufacturing. The neck angle can be slightly
adjusted by tightening or loosening the coordinator rods,
but this process actually pulls the rim out of round and
should only be used for minor adjustments. If the neck
angle is seriously off, the instrument should be taken to a
qualified repair shop to be re-cut.

String gauge affects the playability in two ways. The
heavier the string, the tighter the feel of the instrument
will be. Also the heavier string will put more tension on
the instrument, raising the action.

Maintenance Tips

To keep your banjo happy and healthy, here are some daily habits to develop:

- Wipe down your banjo after you play it. Leaving dirt, grease, and even fingerprints on your instrument for any period of time can permanently damage it. It's best to develop the habit of wiping the fingerprints off the plated metal parts, and wiping the oil and  perspiration off the strings and fingerboard. Specially treated cloths can be purchased to clean metal and finished wood parts of your banjo. These are available on the Deering Banjo website, www.deeringbanjo.com.
  - Avoid vinyl and plastics in shoulder straps and hangers or stands. They contain solvents that react with the finish. Also avoid polishes with silicone or abrasives in them. You can use mirror glaze or toothpaste to rub out light scratches. Just apply with a cotton cloth and rub vigorously. Deeper scratches need the attention of a professional.
- Another good habit to develop is to always latch your case when your banjo is in it. I've repaired many dings and a few broken necks caused by someone picking up an unlatched case and having the instrument spill out on the floor.

Every few months you should:
- Change the strings.
- Rub some graphite in the nut slots.
- Clean and polish the fingerboard and frets with 0000 steel wool.
- Oil the fingerboard with lemon oil or almond stick.
- Check the head tension.
- Check the bridge placement.
- Check the tailpiece adjustment.

And to wrap it up, here is a checklist of things to do to get the best from your banjo:

- Be sure all the hardware is tight to prevent buzzes and rattles.
- Always put on a new set of strings when setting the intonation.
- Be sure the neck is securely tightened to the rim.
- Tighten the thumbscrews, securing the resonator to the flange.
- Check the head tension for tightness and uniformity.
- Be sure the tuner screws are tight.
- Check the placement of the bridge. Also check to see it's not sagging in the middle. Replace it if it is.
- Check the adjustment and alignment of the tailpiece.
- Check the neck relief and adjust the truss rod, if necessary.
- Set the string height to your preference.
- Be sure to check all settings with the banjo tuned to standard pitch.

There are several books and many articles available on the subject of banjo setup and maintenance, and there are great websites to visit for more information. Keep your eyes and ears open, listen to other banjo players, and ask questions. Remember, as you make adjustments, to document your starting point so you can return to that setting should you not be satisfied with the changes you've made. A slight adjustment can make a big difference in sound and playability, so move in incremental steps. Most of all, take the time to become familiar with the workings of the banjo. It will help you develop confidence in your ability to keep your banjo happy and healthy, and will also improve your playing.

Help Desk

If you've gotten all the way here, then you have already figured out that there really isn't a help desk at Blue Mountain Banjo Camp, at least not one that has a person sitting at a desk. (We almost outsourced a real customer service desk in Kuala Lumpur, but were outflanked by a multinational conglomerate.) However, there are four sources of real help available.

First, you'll find a listing of Internet resources, including URLs of publications, camps, and prime banjo websites. Many of the artists in *Banjo Camp!* have pages on MySpace, and a few have videos on YouTube. It's worth a shot.

Next, for free updates, current banjo camp information, downloads, and discussion forums with other Banjo Campers, head on over to the online campus at www.banjocamp.us.

Don't forget to use the Index on page 150: It can help you locate people, songs, and workshops, but probably not any items being held in the Camp's lost-and-found department.

Lastly, and certainly not as a last resort, you are most welcome to e-mail the author, anyone at Lark Books, and every artist and manufacturer mentioned in the book. I can't answer for anyone else, but I will respond since, after finishing this book, I'll be mostly sitting on the porch, playing banjo, and waiting for the mailman to deliver my royalty checks.

You can reach me or Buddy McCoy at genesenyak@bellsouth.net. (In Turkestan and Uzbekistan it's zhenya@bellsouth.net.) And if you're requesting an autographed 8 x 10 black-and-white glossy, please attach a stamped, self-addressed envelope to your e-mail.

This has been a lot of fun. Thanks for attending Blue Mountain Banjo Camp! I hope to get the chance to jam with you one day soon.

☸ ON-LINE RESOURCES

In this post-Google era, presenting a listing of banjo websites might be a bit redundant. But sharing some of my own limited and faltering experiences has been a good part of *Banjo Camp!* so why stop now.

The following sites come out of my own list of favorites, bookmarked for when I'm looking for tabs or news, a piece of equipment, or just an online banjo connection. They provided me unfailing inspiration and practical tips. Included are some favorites of Blue Mountain Banjo Camp teachers.

Here they are along with Internet connections for faculty and friends.

www.banjonews.com
Banjo Newsletter, for old-time and bluegrass, the place to start. (DON'T make the mistake of typing in "banjo newsletter" and expect to get to the real thing.)

www.banjohangout.org
Chat, videos, 1000+ tabs, lists, forums, news, classifieds, private spaces, photos, blog—you know, a hangout only with banjos

www.banjosessions.com
Mel Bay's monster music site. Tabs, articles

www.bluegrassmusic.com
Bluegrass unlimited, reviews, classifieds, surveys

www.thebluegrassblog.com
For all things bluegrass, news, videos, commentary, archives

bluegrassmusicjams.com/index.html
A work in progress, listing bluegrass jams across America

www.jbott.com
Jim Bottorff's banjo site, filled with good alphabetized tabs, clear lessons, chord and progression charts

www.countysales.com
Their unabashed motto: "The world's largest selection of bluegrass and old-time music"

www.oldtimeherald.org
Old-time Herald's focus on Southern Appalachian old-time music is open to all streams feeding into and out of that rich source.

www.ezfolk.com/links/banjo--bluegrass.html
Collection of links

zeppmusic.com/banjo/
Massive Banjo listing from Donald Zepp, covering all aspects of banjo style, tunings, etc., with invaluable articles, tips and chat

www.folkofthewood.com/page5304.htm
Online lessons in bluegrass banjo

For Blue Mountain Banjo Campers

www.banjocamp.us
The one absolutely free banjo camp. Hook up with other *Banjo Camp!* readers worldwide to locate jam partners, exchange opinions, offer advice, locate instruments and supplies, find a teacher, take a lesson, get unmediated opinion on banjo camps. Rated B (interactive site filled with banjo pickers)

✲ FACULTY AND CONTRIBUTORS

Bob Altschuler
www.dyerswitch.com

Bobby Anderson
www.blueridgetradition.com

Blue Ridge Old Time Music Week
www.mhc.edu/oldtimemusic

Laura Boosinger
www.LauraBoosinger.com

Bob Carlin
www.bobcarlinmusic.com

Janet Davis
www.janetdavismusic.com

Wayne Erbsen
www.nativeground.com

Bill Evans
www.nativeandfine.com

Jack Hatfield
www.hatfieldmusic.com

John Herrmann
www.youtube.com

Geoff Hohwald
www.cvls.com

David Holt
www.davidholt.com

Banjo Camp North
www.mugwumps.com

Adam Hurt
www.adamhurt.com

Phil Jamison
www.warren-wilson.edu/~music/faculty.php

Steve Kaufman
www.flatpik.com

Bill Keith
www.beaconbanjo.com

Brad Leftwich
www.tombradalice.com

Alan Munde
www.almundesbanjocollege.com

Tom Nechville
www.nechville.com

Ken Perlman
www.kenperlman.com

Rich Stillman
www.waystation.net

Tony Trischka
www.tonytrischka.com

Pete Wernick
www.drbanjo.com

Todd Wright
www.deeringbanjos.com

Acknowledgments

This is the place to acknowledge my banjo heroes who never made it into Banjo Camp!, who contributed so much through their music and inspiring performances, and yet missed out on all the fun, jam sessions, shindigs, and shenanigans of camp. Thank you to Bela Fleck, Earl Scruggs, Charlie Poole, Don Reno, Charlie Lowe, Ralph Stanley, J.D. Crowe, Fred Cockerham, Steve Martin, Krazy Kat, R. Crumb, the kid from Deliverance, and all the rest of you.

Nothing would have been possible without the genius, the good will and good humor of all the Blue Mountain Banjo Camp faculty and friends. Thank you to Nancy Nitchie, Jan Davidson, J.D. Robinson, Geoff Hohwald, Jack Hatfield, Bill Keith, Sonny Adcock, Butch Robins, James McKinney, Janet Davis, Ken Perlman, Snuffy Smith, Pete and Joan Wernick, Mike Holmes, Todd Wright, Tony Trischka, Alan Munde, Bill Evans, Eric Weissberg, Bob Altschuler, Rich Stillman, Drew Field, Kelly Stockton, Hank Sapoznik, Happy Traum, John Herrmann, Howie Burson, Brad Leftwich, Casey Henry, Steve Kaufman, Laura Boosinger, Bob Carlin, Phil Jamieson, Adam Hurt, Joe Thompson, Rhiannon Giddens, Dom Flemons, Justin Robinson, Wayne Erbsen, Hilary Dirlan, Pete and Toshi Seeger, Rick Sampson, and Tom Nechville.

I have been extraordinarily lucky in my two primary banjo teachers, Bobby Anderson, who opened wide the door to bluegrass, and David Holt, whose specific and excellent clawhammer teaching, enshrined in "Georgia Buck Is Dead," enlightened me to the old-time way.

Thank you to Jackie Allison for all her work on Shindig, to Bobby Fulcher and Wayne Ingram for first coming up with the idea of Banjo Camp, to Don Nitchie for keeping the Banjo Newsletter porch light burning, to Mark Weeg for getting me started picking, to Stephanie Onel for covering Jenny and Bozo while I was out in the banjo camp wilds, and to the Asheville Pack Memorial Library research staff for much help and documentation in pulling together the early history of banjo camps.

A grateful shout-out to Lark book's senior art director, Chris Bryant, and book designer Thom Gaines for the brilliant work they delivered under pressure. Also, a big thank you to the phenomenal work of Grammy award winner, Steven Heller, Upstream Productions, for creating the CD, which may not win a Grammy, but will surely help others along that path.

And then there's my editor at Lark Books, Deborah Morgenthal, who shepherded this book from first presentation right on through to the end, with wit, humor, and a pencil as sharp as a stainless steel banjo thumb pick. If not for her work, none of us would have gone to Blue Mountain Banjo Camp this year.

Finally, there are the bright and hopeful hordes of banjo campers whose images percolate through these pages—and you, dear reader. Banjo Camp! is, after all, your story.

So just keep that banjo in tune and keep on picking, frailing, singing, and dancing. Like Pete says, music is one of the things that will save the world!

Zhenya Gene Senyak
Asheville, North Carolina

Author Bio

Zhenya Gene Senyak spent the bulk of his career translating his first name into a series of Russian-English dictionaries which are widely distributed in Turkistan's famed book stalls. In the course of his book tour he ran across the balalika master Shlomo Pasguhdnik who introduced him to the banjar. From there it was a short step to borrowing the dinars necessary for him to attend an American banjo camp. He won the red flag at one camp, avoided a wedgie at another and sort of graduated to pick and jam on the streets of Hominy Creek, North Carolina, before deciding to write this book to further his education and finance his studies at banjo camps next year. His writings have appeared in a number of national publications, including *The Bialystok Kurier* and *Banjo Newsletter*.

Photo and Illustration Credits

Index

Audio CD Index

Welcome to Banjo Camp! with Zhenya Gene Senyak

Bobby Anderson Beginning Bluegrass

Bobby and the Bluegrass Tradition Jam Tracks

Clawhammer & Old-Time Banjo with David Holt

Bringing It Home with Zhenya Gene Senyak